Dishes
from
Indonesia

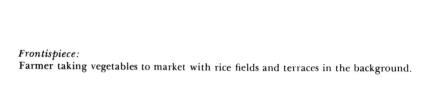

Frontispiece:
Farmer taking vegetables to market with rice fields and terraces in the background.

Dishes
from
Indonesia

by

YOHANNI JOHNS

ELM TREE BOOKS
0 241 89943 5

To
GAEK and NEN,
my grandmothers
IBUNDA DAWIAH,
my mother
MONICA,
my daughter

Thomas Nelson (Australia) Ltd
 19-39, Jeffcott Street,
West Melbourne, AUSTRALIA
First published 1971
new metricated edition 1977
Copyright (c)
Yohanni Johns 1971 Plate 1 (Richard Woldendorp)
ISBN 0241 89943 5

Contents

List of Plates

Foreword

PERHAPS it hardly needs saying that good food is more than a pleasure to the senses or a temptation to gluttony. Eating is a social activity and, in a very real sense, people are not only what they eat, but also how they eat. The ritual of the table is part of a way of life. And in very many societies, the essential values, human wisdom and quality of life of a people are reflected directly or indirectly in those formal meals which mark the major stages of an individual's journey through life, which celebrate the annual cycle of festivals, and which are held to call down a blessing on a new undertaking, or as an act of thanksgiving for peril averted.

The author has written this book with these ideas very much in mind. It is, I think, her special gift to be able to see two styles of life clearly and fully, and to interpret one in terms of the other. It is a quality which she has shown to very good effect as a wife and a mother in the special circumstances of a cross-cultural marriage. It has contributed notably to her career as a language teacher; and in this book it is brought to bear on a new but certainly related area of human activity, social eating. In reading the manuscript, I have again been made conscious of ideas we share: that many things in life are relative; that the values of any one society generally have their counterparts in any other, even if they are expressed in different forms; and that to limit one's experience of life to a single style of living or set of thought patterns results in a certain sterility of personality. In a broader sense, it is only with the interpretation of values and attitudes to life that the study of anything at all has real value; and to understand that identical human concerns may be as carefully structured and guarded in one way of life as another is perhaps the ultimate in empathy. May this book thus contribute something both to better eating and wiser living.

A. H. JOHNS

The Author

EARLY in 1955 when my husband proposed to me, I said to him: 'You'd better think this over carefully, you may regret it later; I can't cook.' What I meant was that he was from England, and I did not know how to cook English food. This may sound amusing, but I was serious. At that time I knew little about England, only what I had learnt from history books and a few novels, and these did not tell me much about the tastes of English gourmets.

I come from a town in Indonesia called Padang Panjang. It is situated in the mountains of West Sumatra and belongs to an area known as Minangkabau. It has a form of social organisation that anthropologists call matrilineal. This has nothing to do with that frightening sounding word matriarchal, which suggests that authority is in the hands of the woman. It only means that ancestral property is passed down in the female line, and that the person responsible for the administration of this property is the eldest brother of the senior woman in the family house. In this society, the husband is given a place in his wife's family house, where the couple have a room for their personal use. In other words, marriage provides a man with a home as well as a wife. This way of life is ruled by a traditional system of law and value called *adat,* which covers almost every aspect of everyday activity and personal relationships. This *adat* is gradually losing its hold but is still something to be reckoned with. When my grandmothers were in their prime (they are now both in their nineties), the traditional way of life was everything. In this traditional way of life, a wife has many duties and responsibilities. There are those she owes her husband, of course, but in addition she has a hundred and one unwritten obligations towards her in-laws and the surrounding community. Her position as a wife is all the more secure if she can keep on good terms with these in-laws and win the respect of the community at large. To do this, she must cheerfully fulfil all these obligations, prominent among which is hospitality. So, if she is a good cook, she has a lot going for her.

Both my grandmothers were anxious to bring up their grand-daughters, myself included, to be ideal wives: good at cooking, sewing, housekeeping, and prudent in their dealings at the market. The world they lived in seems old-fashioned now, but they understood it and their place in it. Indeed, it had a rhythm and a logic of its own, and in the cycle of life of the community they were well known. By and large Indonesian village life has the same qualities of village life anywhere. All the events in the village, whether of the religious or the agricultural year or of the individual's life, are shared by the whole community. For a wedding banquet in the city professional caterers are available; in the country a wedding feast is a village affair. Everything has to be done at home, including the slaughter of the animals, ranging from cows for a major celebration, to goats for a medium-sized one and chickens for a small one. For a week before the great event, friends, neighbours and relations will come to lend a hand, knowing full well that you will do the same for them when the time comes. Some contribute in kind, sending around perhaps a hundred coconuts, a dozen chickens or a supply of vegetables. Others will work grinding chilli, plucking the chickens, cutting vegetables or stirring cauldrons of food. Still more will provide the know-how, and in this my grandmothers were in their element. They were well-known both for their skill as cooks and sense of occasion. Thus they were often in demand. Whenever there was an important wedding, they were often to be seen together, watching the preparations with eagle eyes, tasting the dishes to see how they were coming on, advising what to add, what to do next and the trouble spots to avoid. Given such a background and interests, they could hardly be expected to look on a knowledge of English as a useful qualification for a girl. Rather, they were afraid that too much book learning would put a girl on the shelf, and in a way they were right.

My father, however, was a school inspector who sensed that we were growing up in a time of transition. So he allowed me to go to a Dutch school in addition to receiving the traditional kind of education at home. His only hope was that I should strike a balance between the two ways of life. His own standpoint was simple. He used to say: 'My child, in this town we are part of a community, and have to live accordingly. Even if we think something is right, we should not do it if the community does not accept it.' But in one respect he was prepared to disregard community views, and for this I have always been grateful to him. The townsfolk in those days felt that something was seriously amiss if a girl was still unmarried after she had passed the age of twenty. And for a girl to continue her education after this age was beyond all reason! Yet he stood for my right both to remain single and to study, despite public opinion and the alarm and despondency this caused among my other relatives.

It was with my maternal grandmother that I had most contact. I loved good food and I enjoyed cooking, so during school holidays I would help her in the kitchen. She was a perfectionist, exacting and meticulous in every detail of the preparation, cooking and serving of any dish to which she set her hand. At times it seemed that everything I did was wrong: I did not cut vegetables neatly enough; she told me that the way I cleaned fish, sliced liver, or disjointed poultry was squeamish. Of course, it felt slimy, and I was afraid of spotting my clothes with blood, so I handled the food with my finger-tips, and stood back from the bench. She used to snap at me: 'It's food, not filth, hold it firmly!' Her tongue was sharp, but her heart (and intentions) were kind. Often I went back to my books feeling disgusted with myself, but I always returned the following day to try again. Now, looking back, I realise that she was giving me a thorough grounding in the technique and art of cooking in a way that I could never have learnt from books.

Cooking was one of the subjects taught at the college where I did my teacher training, but it was not a major subject and was Dutch oriented. However, after my graduation I taught English at a Home Economics school, and whenever I was free, attended cooking classes with my senior pupils. Here, I learnt something of the 'academic' approach to cooking.

I was a restless child, always looking for adventure. I wanted to travel and see the world, but being a woman was a very real obstacle. One of my brothers had gone abroad when he was eighteen, and he wrote to me regularly from the great world beyond my town and country. This kept my ambition alive. One of my plans was to get a transfer in the Education Service from Sumatra to Makassar, in the Celebes, over a thousand miles away, where I could stand on my own feet and be myself. Little did I realise what the future held.

In 1954, a new English Teachers' Training College sponsored by the Ford Foundation was opened in Bukittinggi. I applied for enrolment in the two year course and was lucky enough to be selected. Our instructors included four Americans. During the courses we learnt a great deal, not only about the English language and how to teach it, but also about the English and American ways of life, culture and indirectly (perhaps not so indirectly, for food is culture too) about their cuisine. Sometimes they entertained us, and we were very impressed to discover that one of them was a genuine gourmet for whom cooking was a serious hobby. This was my first introduction to American food, and it marked my introduction to world cuisine with a vengeance.

Then, on 11 July 1956, after almost two years of soul searching, I did the most 'imprudent' thing I have ever done, and thus changed the whole course of my life. I married the Englishman who had proposed to me. It is almost impossible to count the reasons why it was imprudent. But many years and five children later there seems to be no cause for regret. Life, if I might put it in culinary terms, has had pungency and bite and a wide variety of flavours and textures supported by a secure base of white rice, representing shared ideals and common purpose. I would not change it for anything . . . but back to my story.

During our honeymoon in England and Europe I felt somewhat like Alice in Wonderland. There were so many new things to be absorbed, and food was no exception. In England I quietly watched my mother-in-law preparing roast beef and Yorkshire pudding. In Paris I took to French cuisine like a duck to water. In Italy I had spaghetti for the first time. The lightness and flavour of the pasta and the marvellously defined taste of the sauces won an enthusiastic response from my tastebuds. Unfortunately, in my enthusiasm I did not realise that this was just a first course, and when the main dish arrived—a wonderfully flavoured veal with cheese—I was unable to do it justice. Still, we learn by mistakes.

Another occasion I remember occurred during a stop-over in Bangkok after a long flight from Rome. After three months in Europe we fancied something different and went out for a walk hoping there would be a local-style restaurant nearby. At the end of a small side street we found what we were looking for. The owner seemed a little surprised, but pleased to see a foreign couple come in, and he did his best for us. For some reason or other the combination of fish and vegetable dishes was both familiar to me as an Indonesian, yet different, and the whole meal, basically a simple one in a simple restaurant, was one I shall never forget.

My stay in Jogjakarta in Central Java (1956-58) marked a new stage in my experience of cuisine. Until my first child was born in 1958, I taught English at a Training College for Domestic Science Teachers. Of course, I could not help hearing a lot about food and recipes, and was often brought the students' work to taste and evaluate. At the same time we belonged to a very international community. There were various overseas organisations sending staff to assist in the development of educational institutions in Jogjakarta. In some ways the situation was paradise for housewives, for domestic help was part of the way of life. For people not brought up in the Javanese tradition, the only regular diversion was that offered by two cinemas. Reciprocal entertainment was an obvious answer, and this brought about the discovery and enjoyment on everyone's part of many kinds of dishes which included local Javanese specialities beside Russian, Greek, Italian, French and a wide range of American styles. These were a far cry from the dishes I had grown up with in my mountain town, although I am sure that these can hold their own with any.

Apart from several round-the-world trips and visits to Indonesia, I have now lived in Australia since 1958. These years have deepened and extended my experience in many ways, and as far as cuisine is concerned, they have taught me that it is as inexhaustible as life itself.

Acknowledgements

THIS BOOK offers a wide but still relatively small selection of dishes from Indonesia. In it I have included dishes I have grown up with, dishes I have enjoyed in various parts of Indonesia, and dishes I have learnt about through discussions with friends or fossicking through old Indonesian cookery books. In many ways, my choice has been personal. There are recipes from all the major islands of Indonesia, recipes which I thought were interesting in their own right, which foreigners would enjoy, and for which the ingredients were generally available in temperate countries. No national cookery book can claim to be complete, and this is no exception.

Many friends—Indonesian, Dutch, Australian, American and Malaysian—have helped me in the preparation of this book. A list of names is always invidious. I hope, therefore, that all those who have helped me will realise my deep appreciation in this general expression of thanks even if I make a special mention of only three names: Mrs Elly H. Soebardi, who made a great deal of information and experience available to me and cheerfully answered telephone queries at any hour of the day or night and to whom must go the credit for the recipe (p. 140) for the Spiced Rich Layer Cake; Mrs Judy Achjadi, who read through the manuscript and made available to me Indonesian reference books not available in Australia, and, last but not least, Miss Milly Rutishauser who typed and retyped my illegible handwriting with an amazing thoughtfulness and percipience.

Doubtless this book has it share of errors and imperfections. These of course are my responsibility alone.

YOHANNI JOHNS

Preparing spices: in the foreground, chillies, candlenuts and lemon grass

1 Background to Indonesian Cooking

EVERY now and then when entertaining European friends, I serve Indonesian food, and the reactions of my guests are often interesting. One may say of my stir-fried vegetables: 'That was good; I had something like it once before at a Chinese friend's place. But it is an Indonesian dish, isn't it?' And another may say of a meat or chicken dish cooked in coconut milk: 'I love curries. When I was in India it was fascinating to watch an Indian friend preparing a curry, carefully grinding and combining spices. I suppose that Indonesian food is prepared in much the same way?' Such comments usually lead to interesting conversations.

Yes, there is a Chinese influence in Indonesian cuisine, because there have been Chinese in Indonesia from the dawn of Indonesian history (the earliest traces of their presence being wall paintings and porcelains from about 200-100 B.C.) and diplomatic relations between China and various Indonesian rulers, some of whom visited China, from the year A.D. 500 onwards. They occupied themselves in many fields of activity, even marrying into the royal families of regional courts. When the Dutch arrived in Banten in 1596, their vessel was surrounded by the little boats of Javanese, Chinese and Gujerati petty traders. In fact, although the Chinese are mostly known for financial skills, they have been fishermen, sailors, bricklayers, carpenters and even farmers. In many areas they participated in the Indonesian way of life, in most respects retaining their group identity as Chinese, yet also becoming Indonesianised. Many modified versions of their dishes are now accepted as Indonesian.

From another part of Asia came Indian culture; the first Hindu kingdom in Indonesia was established by A.D. 400. But the arrival of Muslim Gujerati traders from the Islamic centre of Ahmadabad in north-west India precipitated a more sustained and intense contact both with India and the countries of the Middle East and resulted in the gradual Islamisation of Indonesia.

One of the most important Muslim institutions is the pilgrimage to the shrine in Mecca, the Kaaba, on the twelfth month of the

Preparing coconut milk

Muslim year. Over the centuries this institution has brought together Muslims from all over the world, including Indonesia, some of whom have remained for months or even years in the Holy City and travelled in Egypt, Syria and Irak before returning home. The Indian and Arab styles of cooking found their way into Indonesian cuisine through the religious associations of Muslim, Indian and Arab cultures.

It goes without saying that the three hundred years of Dutch presence in Indonesia and the close association between the Dutch and Indonesian peoples also left a mark on Indonesian cooking. In spite of all these outside influences, Indonesian cuisine in its various forms still retains features all its own.

Indonesia is a large country, consisting of thousands of islands, large and small, which vary widely from region to region in people, language, customs and natural resources. Indonesian cooking reflects this variety. In this book I have included only the recipes with which I am familiar, e.g. from Java, Bali, Sumatra and Celebes. These differ not so much in the cooking methods as in the way various seasonings, spices and sauces are combined. In Java, for example (especially Central Java), a large amount of brown sugar (palm sugar) is used in most dishes. Whenever soya sauce is used, the dark sweet variety with the caramel added to it is frequently preferred. As a contrast to the sweetness of the dishes, pickled bird eye chillies are very popular, and sometimes a few are added to vegetables or the meat dish itself. Shrimp paste and salam leaves are widely used.

In Sumatra, however, especially Central Sumatra, even though this region is known throughout the archipelago for the pungency of its dishes, bird eye chillies are seldom used, and sugar in meat, fish or chicken dishes is unheard of. As for shrimp paste—it is only used for vegetable dishes or sambals to give a tasty fish flavour, and hardly ever added to meat, chicken or fish dishes, with the exception of stir-fried-type dishes (*Sambal goreng*). Ginger is widely used.

In Bali, shrimp paste and soya sauce are used a great deal and this island is well known for its pork dishes. In fact, wherever you are in Bali, you have only to walk a few yards before being greeted by snorting pigs.

From the little I know of the dishes from Celebes, I can only comment that they seldom use sugar except in certain salad-type dishes and for sweet and sours.

Although some regional styles are included in the recipes in this book, it is sometimes difficult to indicate places of origin. In many cases this would be impossible, since the dishes have been adapted and modified many times over the years.

WAYS AND MEANS

When I look back and consider how the majority of Indonesian housewives, using traditional utensils, had to spend hours at a time in their kitchens preparing family meals, and then reflect on the variety of labour-saving devices available in the modern kitchens of industrialised countries, I marvel that such wonderful dishes could be produced with such primitive implements.

The most important piece of equipment in the traditional Indonesian kitchen is the round, solid grinding stone, on which chillies, coriander seeds and other spices are ground for long hours with a pestle until they are reduced to a smooth paste. In most cases the same result can be achieved in a fraction of the time by using an electric blender, although it may be necessary to add some liquid in order to keep all the ingredients moving—oil, if the paste is to be fried, or water, if it is to be added to coconut milk or stock. Naturally you should check the procedure in the method given in the recipe. If oil has been added to the blender, then it is not necessary to add extra oil to the heated pan prepared for frying the paste. Even so, there are times when I would not be without my grinding stones, as, for example, when I need to prepare very small quantities of dry spices, or to make particular sambals such as shrimp-paste sambal (page 102) or steamed sambal (page 102).

Another utensil that the Indonesian cook cannot be without is the wok (kuali), a kind of large, round, bowl-shaped frying pan with a curved base. These are now generally available here made from various metals—copper or iron, aluminium or stainless steel. Some manufacturers produce a model with a lid. This wok is a most versatile cooking utensil. Since it is thin, it heats quickly; its shape provides a cooking surface of maximum size and distributes the heat evenly. It is therefore ideal for stir-frying, but just as useful for poaching or frying eggs and, since the surface is round, even if an egg breaks it does not loose its shape. The slanting sides make it easy to turn food over, so that it is simpler to make pancakes or omelettes in one than in a conventional frying pan. It is also good for dry-frying ingredients such as grated coconut, coriander, caraway seeds and so on. The model with the lid can be used for steaming. It is necessary only to half fill the wok with water, place in it the heatproof dish or tin containing the food to be cooked on a steaming rack (a metal ring), then cover the wok. The circulating steam is a particularly effective cooking agent. If a particular dish needs a long period of cooking, it is necessary to check the water level from time to time, adding water as necessary, otherwise the steam may not be sufficient. Woks come in all sizes, from the mini wok of about 10 cm (4 inches) in diameter to the maxi which is large enough for a goat!

There is, however, a catch. A wok cannot be used effectively on the hot plate of an electric stove. I have been told that it functions well over a gas burner, provided that it is set on a metal frame to keep it steady. Here, the Indonesian way of cooking has its advantage, since either open charcoal stoves or kerosene burners over which the wok fits are used. And even the most elementary method of cooking, using three hearthstones on which to set the wok, does a very good job. The basic idea is that a major area of the bottom part of the wok should be directly exposed to the heat so that the whole wok is heated quickly.

Despite all the uses of the wok however, an electric frying pan is adequate in most cases, but I sometimes wish that they could be designed in the shape of a wok to make stirring easier!

Certain types of banana leaves, whether light green young ones or dark green old ones, can rightly be regarded as cooking utensils in Indonesia, and are sold in the markets for this purpose. Before use they are wilted by exposure to heat or sunlight. They are used for wrapping sweetmeats and certain fish dishes or vegetables before grilling or steaming. They have the same kind of function as foil, with the important difference that they contribute sometimes to colouring as well as appearance. Moreover, since the leaves are pliable, they can be folded into various shapes which identify the contents. The wrapping and folding of ingredients to be cooked is meticulously done before they are steamed or cooked on charcoal, as the case may be. Of course, the banana leaves are not to be eaten.

Another useful implement is a wire grill-holder, large enough to take a splayed open chicken or a whole 1.5 kg (3 pound) fish. This is ideal for grilling over charcoal. It makes turning easy, and there is no danger of dropping or breaking the chicken or fish, as the case may be. Such holders are now available in this country for use on barbecues or fishing trips.

Good cooking depends to a large measure on attention to detail, and this includes the preparation, whether for meat or vegetable dishes, such as cutting. In determining how to cut vegetables, the considerations are the nature of the vegetable, how it is to be cooked (e.g. boiled, stir-fried, cooked in coconut milk), the ingredients to be combined and so on. These are only a few examples of many ways of cutting certain vegetables. Others are clearly described in the recipes. Whether sliced, cut or cubed, the ingredients for any given dish should be cut uniformly so that they cook evenly.

Boiling
—Cabbage is either cut into large wedges or left whole after removing discoloured outer leaves (see page 30).
—Young beans are topped, tailed and slit.
—Choko is peeled, cored and cut into quarters lengthwise.
—Bamboo shoots are cut into very thin slices across the grain, then cut into pieces 5 cm (2 inches) square. The same method applies if they are to be cooked in coconut milk (see page 31).

Stir-frying
The general rule is that the ingredients are cut into small pieces for easy stirring.
—Cabbage is finely sliced into strips.
—Beans are sliced either diagonally or crosswise into 2.5 cm (1-inch) lengths.
—Choko are usually cut into cubes or match-sticks.
—Bamboo shoots are thinly sliced or cut into match-sticks.

In the preparation of these recipes I have sometimes found classification a little difficult. In certain cases it is difficult to say where a meat dish ends and a vegetable one begins, because a small quantity of meat may be used to flavour particular vegetable dishes. The meat to be used in such dishes is usually cut into cubes or shredded, either to match or contrast with the shapes of the vegetables with which it is to be cooked. Dishes of this kind I have regarded as vegetable. For meat dishes proper, the meat is usually cut into pieces (if it is not to be cooked in the piece) of not less than 5 cm (2 inches) square, each piece forming a notional helping.

WHAT IS RIJST-TAFEL?
The *Rijst-tafel* (or Rice Table) is a high spot of almost all pre-war travel literature in Indonesia. Aldous Huxley, in a celebrated passage, describes his experience of it as follows:

"Ane Rice Tafel for mich", you say, combining German and lowland Scotch into what you believe, quite erroneously, to be the language of

Holland . . . you wait . . . A waiter appears at your elbow with an enormous cauldron of rice; you heap your plate with it. He moves away. Immediately another takes his place, offering fish soup. You dampen your rice; the soup man goes. A dish of chops at once replaces the tureen. Looking around, you see that the chop carrier is standing at the head of a long procession of Javanese waiters, extending in unbroken line from your table right across the dining-room to the kitchen door. Each time you help yourself, the procession advances a step, and a new dish is presented. I took the trouble one day to count the number of dishes offered to me. Twenty-six actually appeared before me; but it was a busy day for the waiters, and I do not think I got all the dishes I was entitled to. They included after the chops two other kinds of meat; two kinds of birds; a species of sausage; fish, both fresh and dried; roast bananas; several kinds of vegetables, plain and curried; two varieties of salad; fried nuts; numerous pickles and jam; a queer kind of unleavened bread, and various other things which I cannot at the moment remember.

How did such an institution—for institution it is rather than a mere meal—develop? To understand this, it is necessary to know something of Indonesian life and Indonesian attitudes to their Dutch rulers.

Variety of choice is the key-note of Indonesian hospitality and a mark of honour to a guest. The more important the guest, the greater the variety of dishes that should be available, the philosophy being that if there is one that the guest does not like, there will be another that he does. In the early days of their rule in Java, the Dutch learnt to live in the style of and to expect the respect due to princes and one can imagine the long procession of servants hovering around their master with numerous dishes, ready with cucumber or sliced banana to sooth the great man's tongue if inadvertently he took too large a mouthful of chilli.

As for the name, it is quite likely that it was a convenient term to distinguish Indonesian-style food from *Hollands eten* (Dutch-style) food, because in a general sense all Indonesian meals are 'rice-tables', whatever the combinations of dishes that go with the boiled or steamed rice. The same could be said of many Indian and Chinese dishes. However, over the years the variety and style of the dishes evolved into the colonial ritual meal Huxley describes. Today however, it is mostly used in Dutch restaurants to indicate an Indonesian menu, interesting no doubt, but nothing like as sumptuous as was the high colonial-style rice-table.

Indonesian restaurants have been growing in popularity overseas during the past ten years and all of them include 'rice-table' in their menus. This item usually consists of boiled rice accompanied by three or four meat-type dishes, two or three side-dishes, two or three vegetable dishes, one egg dish and of course, sambal. All the various constituents are presented in small oval-shaped dishes. As a rule the table is cramped, the visual effect is unattractive, and since the quantities are small, the food is usually lukewarm (at best) by the time it reaches the table and cold by the time the diner has decided what he will eat first. In fact, such variety in a meal is quite impractical, especially for inexperienced diners, unless it is done on a grand scale and served by a veritable army of waiters in the way Huxley describes.

An Indonesian family for an everyday meal is normally served five or six dishes at the most: boiled rice, one meat dish, a chicken or fish dish or two vegetables and two side-dishes, and this should be the general principle behind the structure of a menu. This ensures that there is order, not chaos, in the dishes served and that the taste and appearance of each dish is utilised to the best effect. It is with this in mind that I have set out a few sample menus which are popular both in Indonesian homes and restaurants.

MENUS

I

White Rice	Nasi putih (p. 22)
Stir-fried Green Beans	Sambal goreng buncis (p. 38)
Chicken in Mild Sauce	Opor ayam (p. 92)
Meat and Potato Croquettes	Pergedel (p. 108)
Roasted Coconut with Peanuts	Serundeng (p. 109)
Prawn Crackers	Krupuk udang (p. 104)
Shrimp Paste Sambal	Sambal terasi (p. 102)

II

White Rice	Nasi putih (p. 22)
Stir-fried Spinach	Tumis bayam (p. 33)
Curried Eggs and Prawns	Kari telur dengan udang (p. 56)
Fried Eggplant	Goreng terung (p. 44)
Cucumber Pickle	Acar bening ketimun (p. 106)
Prawn Crackers	Krupuk udang (p. 104)
Steamed Sambal	Sambal lada uap (p. 102)

III

White Rice	Nasi putih (p. 22)
Mixed Vegetables in Coconut Milk	Sayur lodeh (p. 39)
Rendang	Rendang (p. 81)
Fried Fish with Tangy Dressing	Ikan acar kuning (p. 61)
Crisp Coconut Sambal	Sambal kelapa kering (p. 100)
Beef or Pork Crackling	Krupuk jangat (p. 104)

IV

White Rice	Nasi putih (p. 22)
Mixed Vegetable Relish	Acar kuning (p. 40)
Spread-eagled Spiced Chicken	Singgang ayam (p. 96)
Broccoli Cooked Sumatran-style	Brokoli gulai pakis (p. 46)
Nut Crackers	Emping (p. 105)

V

White Rice	Nasi putih (p. 22)
Mixed Vegetable Salad	Pecal (p. 42)
Braised Beef Slices	Lapis daging (p. 78)
Potato Omelette	Dadar telur kentang (p. 50)
Peanut Crackers	Rempeyek (p. 105)

HOW TO SERVE AND EAT

After studying the menus and (hopefully) finding them interesting, you will then face the problem of how to prepare and serve the meal. The first thing to remember is that Indonesian meals are not served as separate courses, and all the dishes given are eaten with rice. The rice supplies the bulk of the meal, and its blandness is ideal for absorbing and combining the various flavours of the meat and vegetable dishes, and for a background against which to savour the contrasting tastes and textures.

You may wonder how it is possible or even practical to prepare five or six dishes for a single meal. Yet this is exactly the point. It is not necessary to think in terms of a single meal, particularly as far as meat and poultry dishes are concerned, for their flavour improves over two or three days, and with a refrigerator, there is no problem of their 'going off'.

Since the preparation of side-dishes can take just as long as that of the main dishes, I usually begin to prepare an elaborate meal two or three days in advance. Even though side-dishes, in most cases, complement the meal, beginners may regard them as optional.

Confidence is as important in cooking as it is in riding a bicycle. If you are adventurous, you'll find that you will soon get the knack of coping with unfamiliar dishes. I remember my own experience with a traditional Christmas dinner. I was particularly anxious as to how the white sauce would turn out. Either by luck or good judgment, it turned out well, and this gave me the confidence to tackle various kinds of sauces and other unfamiliar dishes.

In Indonesia, it is not usual to wait for everyone at the table to finish before second helpings are taken. And during a family meal, mother will glance around and quietly pass a dish to anyone whose plate is almost empty. When entertaining, the hostess quickly passes a dish she thinks the particular guest will enjoy when she sees that he is ready for an additional helping. And you will notice that she is always the last to finish. This is not because she is the biggest eater, but because she wishes her guests to feel at ease: not embarrassed if they are naturally slow eaters, or reluctant to take additional helpings if they happen to be hearty eaters.

Sometimes the question arises as to what to drink with this type of food. Often, Indonesians will drink Indonesian tea or iced water. This does not exclude beer, a noteworthy cultural gift from the Dutch. In fact a well-chilled light beer is an ideal accompaniment if richer and more pungent dishes dominate the meal. Otherwise a light wine is very acceptable. One of my favourites is a well-chilled rosé, of the Kaiser Stuhl type, but some people may prefer a white wine with a very slightly astringent flavour—perhaps a fine hock.

Traditionally, Indonesians eat with the fingers of the right hand. Although the use of spoon and fork is very common now, on ceremonial occasions it is usual to revert to tradition. At such meals, each diner is provided with a finger-bowl. This is not to wash off physical dirt (this degree of hygiene is assumed before guests sit down to a meal), but rather to moisten the fingers before eating, so that the rice will not stick to them. There is as much art in the neat and effective use of the fingers as in the use of chopsticks. Food is neither dropped clumsily, nor is it smeared around the outside of the mouth. It is formed into small balls and placed into the mouth. No trace of food should touch the palm of the hand and the fingers should not enter the mouth. It must be stressed that food is never taken with the left hand, and no person with any sense of politeness would pass or take anything with his left hand. When spoon, fork and knife are used, the spoon is held in the right hand, the fork in the left. The knife is used only to cut inconveniently large pieces of meat and is laid on a knife rest beside the diner's plate when not in use (very formal usage).

It is not usual for salt and pepper to be on the table. All the condiments and spices have been added during cooking. Not only would any addition of salt at the table be ineffective, but to ask for it would be to reflect rather pointedly on the hostess's skill as a cook and would, in effect, be rather impolite.

GLOSSARY OF INGREDIENTS

Agar-agar is a kind of gelatine made of seaweed. It is prepared principally in Japan, but is also locally available in Indonesia. Used for the preparation of a sort of gelatine dessert, it takes longer to dissolve than gelatine, but sets very quickly. It is completely tasteless so there are no limits to the flavours you can blend with it for your dessert. It is sold in large stores in different forms, such as blocks and sticks, and in very fine strips like hair.

Bamboo Shoots are the young shoots of bamboo which are just appearing above the ground. Used as a vegetable in stir-fried dishes, it combines well with almost any meat, fish, egg or poultry dish because of its delicacy, crispness and sweetness. In Indonesia they are available fresh all through the year. The fresh variety must be skinned and parboiled for two hours. In Australia they are available in tins and come either whole or in chunks. They should always be rinsed before being used. They are of an ivory colour, rather crunchy and are usually cut uniformly into shapes to match accompanying ingredients. Tinned bamboo shoots require very little cooking, but should be boiled briskly to get rid of the tinny flavour.

Bean Curd, made from soya beans, is considered highly nourishing. It is sold in several forms. The type used in Indonesian cooking is in cake form about three or four inches square, one inch thick. Since it is already cooked, it requires very little cooking. It is extremely versatile; it can be boiled, steamed, stir-fried, deep-fried or eaten fresh. Fried bean curd has a mild nutty flavour, slightly bitter, like walnuts, which lingers on the tongue; the mildness makes it an excellent base for stronger flavours of many kinds.

Bean Sprouts are sprouted from Chinese beans, which are soaked until they germinate. They produce a white shoot, the bean itself remaining as a kind of head to which the original skin is loosely attached. These skins should be removed. Bean sprouts are available fresh or tinned and must be rinsed in cold water before being used. I like to grow my own bean sprouts, and prefer them three or four days old. Below is my method for sprouting the beans.

TO GROW BEAN SPROUTS
Put 125 g ($\frac{1}{4}$ pound) Chinese green beans into bowl, cover with water, let soak for 24 hours. When the skin breaks, strain into a colander; let stand in covered colander in a dark place. Wet beans thoroughly every two or three hours. At night, before going to bed, water beans again. The sprouts should look white and fresh, not brown. Repeat this for three days. Put beans into big saucepan or bowl filled with cold water, stir. Skins will come to surface and can be scooped out with a strainer. Repeat process until all skin is off; the last few bean skins may need to be picked out by hand.

Black Bean Sauce or salted black beans (*tauco*) are in fact preserved soya beans. They are extremely strong, pungent and salty, and used together with garlic as a seasoning to enhance the flavour of meat and vegetables; they modify or subdue the strong flavour of fish. They are available in tins or jars in Continental delicatessens or in large stores specialising in Oriental food.

Candlenuts (Kemiri buah keras) are oily, have very hard shells, and come from the candleberry tree. They should be ground to a fine paste before use. They give a delightful nutty flavour to many Indonesian dishes.

Macadamia nuts or any fatty, oily nuts can be substituted for candlenuts. They are usually available in large stores specialising in Oriental food.

Celeriac (celery root, knob celery, root celery or turnip-rooted celery) is celery that has been developed in part of Australia, America and Europe for the *root* instead of the top. It grows more slowly than celery and is harvested whenever the root is large enough. In Indonesia it is grown for the top or leaves for seasonings and referred to simply as 'celery'. Since celeriac is not always available in this country, I use the top of the locally available celery.
NOTE: Celeriac root can be eaten raw. Peel, cut into fine strips and mix in a bowl with mayonnaise.

Chillies are available fresh from many greengrocers during the summer months. They vary considerably in size and hotness. The smaller the chilli and the thinner the skin, the hotter it tastes. Not all chillies are hot; therefore, whenever I purchase chillies, I usually bite off the tip to find out the hotness of it. Chillies can be ground, seeds and all, by putting them through a mincer a few times or whirling in a blender with a little water for about 40-50 seconds to make a fine paste. Most recipes in this book call for chilli which is hot, and, if not stated, seeds are included. There are two types of ground chilli required in the recipes, coarse and very fine.

Chilli is also used in diagonally-sliced strips, one or two at a time, in stir-fried vegetables for flavour and colour or whole in boiled vegetables or pickles. If fresh chillies are not available, there is a firm which markets a preparation called *Sambal Oelek*. This is a semi-fine chilli paste with only salt added. It can therefore be used wherever chilli is required. This should not be confused with *Sambal Bajak* which is highly spiced and not suitable for cooking. And, of course, sometimes there is dried chilli available in stores specialising in Oriental food. For stir-fried dishes that require sliced chilli, capsicum can be substituted.

Chinese Cabbage is a vegetable with large, curly dark green leaves and long smooth milk-white stems which are firmly closed together forming a firm thick bunch. It is extremely versatile and popular. It also has yellow flowerets which grow from the heart of the cabbage and are particularly tender and delicate. It is available in Chinese grocery shops.

Chinese Peas, Snow Peas (Arcis, kacang kapri) are very young peas. In Indonesia, peas are rarely grown to maturity, but are picked while the pods are still green and tender. The pods as well as the peas are then cooked and eaten. They have a very delicate texture and subtle taste. They are sold fresh by the pound in Chinese grocery stores in big cities.

Cinnamon In some recipes in this book cinnamon sticks (or quills) as well as powdered cinnamon are used. One or two of these quills are used for meat dishes, rice dishes etcetera, for flavouring, but are not eaten. I prefer to use the thin cinnamon bark rather than the thick.

Freshly Grated Coconut To prepare freshly grated coconut, which is sometimes used in the preparation of vegetable dishes and sweets, follow steps I-III for the preparation of coconut milk from the flesh of fresh coconuts (see p. 16). Remove the brown skin from the back of the coconut flesh, then grate.

How to Make Coconut Butter Brown freshly grated or desiccated coconut in a frying pan on low heat stirring constantly. Remove from heat. While hot, grind to a smooth paste. It is this coconut butter which gives the unique and characteristic flavour to curry dishes.

Coriander (Ketumbar) is available in supermarkets in seed or powdered form. In Indonesia coriander and caraway seeds are usually dry-roasted for about 5 minutes on a low heat before they are ground, to bring out the flavour and aroma.

Cummin Seed (jintan) has a pungent flavour and strong aromatic scent and is often used in combination with coriander in the proportion of 1 : 5; they complement each other very well. In Indonesia, cummin and coriander seeds are usually dry-roasted for a few minutes on a low heat to bring out the flavour and aroma before they are ground.

Garlic belongs to the onion family, is used extensively in Indonesian dishes for seasoning meat, seafood, poultry and vegetables. Often it is used finely chopped or minced and cooked directly in hot oil to bring out its flavour. But not only the flavour; for example, while grilling a chicken seasoned with garlic, the aroma coming from the kitchen is indescribably delicious and very inviting.

Ginger Root When fresh, it has a hot, spicy taste. It has a light brown, flaky skin. Ginger is indigenous to Indonesia, China and India. In Indonesian cooking it is essential that the ginger used should be fresh; if not available, the only substitute is dried ginger, which must be soaked before using. Sometimes it is available in tins. It is possible to store ginger by placing it, unwashed, in a plastic bag in the deep freeze. Slice while still frozen. It will keep about two or three weeks in a vegetable crisper in the refrigerator.

Kencur is a root spice, like turmeric, ginger and *laos,* but is little used. In fact, in this book, I suggest it only once (see p. 42, *Pecal*). One notices it when its there, but the flavour is not missed when omitted. However, it is available in dried form under the name *kencur*.

Laos or Lengkuas is a ginger-like root, much used in Indonesian cooking. When a few fresh slices are added to the other ingredients, the resulting combination adds an exotic flavour to chicken, meat, fish and vegetables alike. It is available in powdered form in this country, distributed by Conimex under the name *laos*. In Indonesia, of course, it is used fresh. I must confess that it is a spice I find unsatisfactory in powdered form, and if it is not available fresh, I omit it. But this is a matter of individual taste.

Lemon Grass (Serai) This is a tropical kind of grass with a bulbous root and thin bladelike leaves, with a slight fragrance of lemon about it. Usually just the bottom 10 cm (3 or 4 inches) of the stalk is added whole to flavour a dish. Lemon peel or grated lemon rind can be substituted for lemon grass. Lemon grass grows well in Australia—I grow it in my garden in Canberra, and it even survives the severe winter, but the plant does not grow as tall and big as in the tropics.

Lemon or Lime Leaves are useful substitutes for citrus leaves to flavour many Indonesian dishes.

Macadamia Nut (Waratah family) is widely regarded as superior to any other nut. It is a native of the north coast of New South Wales and southern Queensland. I use it a lot in my recipes as a substitute for candlenuts.

Monosodium Glutamate or Ve-tsin is derived from vegetable sources. It has been known to the Chinese and Japanese for hundreds of years, its original source being seaweed. In Indonesia it is used in many varieties of dishes as a matter of course. Its purpose is to bring out the flavour of the food to which it is added; it does not have any flavour of its own. It is available in this country under various proprietary names, such as *Aji no Moto* (made in Japan), which means 'essence of taste'. Ve-tsin is the proprietary name of monosodium glutamate (made in Hong Kong) and sold in supermarkets in crystal and powder form.

Nutmeg is widely known and readily available in powder form. In Indonesia, however, like all other spices, it is freshly grated before use. There is no doubt that this improves the flavour and aroma.

Oil, Cooking Fat Traditional Indonesian cooking almost exclusively uses *coconut oil* for deep-frying and stir-frying and, when available, *ghee* (purified, or clarified butter) is used for particular dishes. Lard is hardly ever used. This is because it is a product of the pig and is thus unlawful to Muslims.

In this country I use tasteless vegetable oils, i.e. those made from peanuts, corn, cotton seeds, poppy seeds or other similar ingredients. Olive oil, which dominates Italian cooking, has too much character for the taste of Indonesian food. For some dishes I occasionally also use butter or margarine. In the case of butter, any gastronome will tell you that whenever you heat it for a sauté or stir-fry, it is important to watch for the point at which to add the first ingredients (garlic, onions, etcetera). This is immediately *after the slight frothing of the melted butter has subsided*. If left longer, it turns brown. This discolours the ingredients and gives them a burnt taste.

Palm Sugar is marketed here under the name of *Gula Jawa* and in Malaysia is referred to as *Gula Melaka*. It is made from various palms, and is usually prepared in the form of round cakes. It is available in this country in two-ounce packages. Since it is very expensive, I usually mix it with brown sugar when preparing sweets. If at all possible, I never omit it or use a substitute, because the contribution it makes to the sweet in which it is used is unique.

Pandanus The Pandanus (or *Pandan*) is a long, dark green sword-shaped leaf. It is used a great deal in Indonesian sweets for its fragrant scent and its distinctive taste. A few pieces about 5 cm (2 inches) long are added to syrups or sauces and coconut rice for flavour. Sometimes the leaves are pounded, mixed with water and put through a strainer. The liquid is then stirred into various doughs to give a light green colouring as well as to enhance the taste. They may be finely shredded and mixed with petals of different flowers (called *bunga rampai*), assorted scented flowers, used in religious or traditional ceremonies or even scattered in ladies' wardrobes to sweeten the smell of the clothing.

Prawns, Dried These are usually sun-dried and are widely used to give a fish flavouring to vegetable dishes and sambals. They are usually soaked, then chopped or pounded before use. Follow recipes. Ground dried prawns are also available.

Rice (p. 20)
Glutinous Rice is another type of rice used in some of the recipes in this book. Its appearance is slightly different from ordinary rice, the grain being rounder, plumper and cream-coloured; when cooked, it is sticky. It is rich and filling and only a little at a time can be eaten.

Rice Flour made from both ordinary and glutinous rice is also used in some of the recipes. Both kinds are available at Chinese grocery stores.

Salam Leaves are widely used in Indonesian cooking, but unfortunately not always available in this country. Some cookery books suggest bay or curry leaves as a substitute. After testing them in the recipes where they are suggested, I have decided that the authenticity of the dish is better preserved if the salam leaf is simply omitted. Since in Indonesia this ingredient is often used in dried form, I am hoping that it will soon be as readily available here as the other spices.

Shallots are members of the onion family which have a delicate flavour and a very mild garlic sort of taste. They are used extensively in Indonesian cooking, i.e. in vegetable dishes, croquettes, stuffing, fried rice, noodle dishes and general cooking to give a mild onion taste as well as to add colour. As a substitute, you may use spring onions. These are ordinary onions pulled out of the beds before maturity is reached.

Shrimp paste (Blacan, terasi) is made from prawns and has a very strong fishy smell and anchovy-like flavour. It should be used in very small quantities only. Not every western foreigner likes it at once.

Soya Sauce is made from soya beans, wheat, yeast and salt. Originally from China, but used in Indonesia in many dishes to enhance the flavour of meat, poultry, fish and vegetables, it adds colour and flavour to gravies, sauces, marinades and dips. It is available in many grades and varieties, ranging in colour from light to dark and heavy, in consistency from thin to thick. Light soya is light in colour and delicate. It is used in dishes for flavour. Dark soya is blacker, richer and thicker (made from the same ingredients with the addition of caramel). This is used in cooking when both flavour and colour are required. You will find many brands on the market; best are Oriental imports. Some experimenting is necessary to decide on that which appeals most to your taste.

Star Fruit (Belimbing) There are several varieties of star fruit in Indonesia, varying in size from as small as a finger to as large as a medium-sized cucumber. The large ones are juicy and may be either sweet or tasteless. The small ones *(belimbing wuluh)* are very sour, like lemons, and are often cooked with fish. When not available, lemon cut into thin wedges is a good substitute. The star fruit has five sections, and when cut crosswise the section is star-shaped, hence the name.

Tamarind (Asam Jawa), a kind of fruit that has a pleasing sweet and sour flavour, is available in dried form in big stores. The colour is dark brown. The juice is obtained by soaking a small quantity (about 2 tablespoons) in $\frac{1}{4}$ cup of warm water, kneading until softened and then squeezing through a strainer. Lemon juice or vinegar can be substituted for tamarind.

Turmeric (Kunyit) is a kind of root used as a condiment and for colouring because of its high content of bright yellow dye. It is available in powder form in supermarkets. In Indonesia the leaves are also used for certain dishes because of their aroma and flavouring.

COCONUT MILK

To the readers of stories like *Coral Island* and popular travel literature generally about visits to the Indies or South Pacific, coconut milk means the delicious fluid inside a young coconut which is so refreshing after a day's hiking or an excursion, particularly when there are small boys at hand who for a few cents will clamber up a tree to get a choice fresh coconut.

In these recipes, however, the term coconut milk means something different. It is the ingredient that gives exotic flavour to many Oriental dishes, including dishes from Indonesia. It is a tricky thing and on no account may liberties be taken with it; this holds both for its preparation and cooking. In Indonesia it is prepared by grating and soaking in warm water the flesh of fresh coconuts, then straining after squeezing and squeezing it to make the milk come out. The stronger you squeeze, the more milk you get.

However, even in areas where fresh coconuts are readily available, busy housewives interested in trying Indonesian dishes will find it simpler to prepare the milk from desiccated coconut for shelling and grating the coconut flesh involves peril to knuckles and nails as well as being time-consuming and exhausting, even though a blender is of some help.

Coconut milk can be prepared in three styles, very thick, thick, and thin, by soaking desiccated coconut in hot water and squeezing it by hand.

TYPE I

Soak 250 g ($\frac{1}{2}$ pound) of desiccated coconut in $2\frac{1}{2}$ cups of boiling water. Let it stand to cool till it is bearable to the touch. Squeeze thoroughly, as hard as you can, to reconstitute the milk. Strain through a piece of muslin. This yields about 2 cups or more of *very thick coconut milk*. This is called the first squeeze. This style is often used in preparing sweets or to be added in the later stage of cooking.

TYPE II

Soak the same desiccated coconut again for a second squeeze in 3 cups of warm water. Repeat the above process (remember, the rich part has been extracted). This yields about 3 cups of *thin coconut milk*. This type is used to parboil tough meat or some vegetables which require long first squeeze. This style is often used in preparing sweets or added in the later stage of cooking.

TYPE III

If these two liquids are mixed together, the result is *thick coconut milk*. Unless otherwise stated, this is the type used in the recipes in this book. 250 g ($\frac{1}{2}$ pound) desiccated coconut yields about 4 cups thick coconut milk sufficient to cook 1.5 kg (3 pounds) of chicken or the same quantity of beef.

Preparing Coconut Milk with the Blender

I reconstitute coconut milk (type III) from desiccated coconut with a blender. The result is about the same as squeezing by hand, only creamier and much quicker; however, with the average-sized blender only 125 g ($\frac{1}{2}$ pound) can be treated at a time.

Place 250 g ($\frac{1}{2}$ pound) desiccated coconut in 4 cups of hot water (bearable to the touch) in blender and switch to medium speed for 30 seconds. Strain through a piece of muslin. This yields about 4 cups of milk.

If you wish, you can also prepare coconut milk from the flesh of fresh coconut by using a blender. Follow the instructions below:

1 Pierce the three soft 'eyes' at the top of the coconut with a sharp instrument to drain the fluid.

2 Tap the coconut with the back of a chopper or hammer around the circumference until the hard shell cracks and the nut breaks into two halves.

3 Insert the tip of a knife between the shell and the flesh of the nut along the edge of the shell and prize off the flesh. (NOTE: For biscuits, cakes and puddings remove brown skin covering the coconut flesh so that you get a pure white milk without odd little patches of brown debris floating on top. But do not remove this skin if the milk is for meat or vegetable dishes, as it adds significantly to the flavour.)

4 Chop flesh into small pieces.

5 Place half the coconut flesh in a blender with the required warm water (about 2 cups) and switch on for 30 seconds at medium speed.

6 Squeeze through a piece of fine muslin or a fine sieve. Repeat the process with the other half. One good-sized coconut will yield about 4 cups of thick coconut milk (type III). Add less water for very thick coconut milk (type I).

The simplest method, but one which the connoisseur would rarely use, *is to reconstitute commercially available coconut cream.*

The reason for this is as follows:

As coconut milk is cooked, its nature changes. First it becomes thick and smooth, provided that it is stirred continuously to prevent it from curdling. By continued cooking, it becomes thicker and creamier and then oil begins to appear. If it is cooked long enough, coconut milk becomes oil, leaving a deposit at the bottom of the pan.

The flavour changes likewise according to these stages. In some cases, especially vegetable dishes, the cooking time required is only up to the first stage. The taste is smooth, sweet, fresh and delicate.

Other dishes require longer cooking, up to the point when the oil is just beginning to appear. The taste is smooth, rich and creamy.

For one very famous dish called *Rendang,* from Minangkabau where coconut milk takes an important rôle, I certainly insist on using coconut milk either prepared from desiccated coconut or, if possible, fresh coconut. A very long time of cooking on a very low flame is required for this dish until all the liquid is absorbed by the meat which turns a very dark brown and is covered with a tasty residue. The taste is rich, crisp and lingers on the tongue.

Because of the manufacturing process, it is not possible to get from the commercial product the sweet, fresh and delicate flavour of the first stage, the smooth, rich and creamy taste and so on; and in my experience it is also rough, has a slightly soapy and sometimes even stale flavour.

When cooking with coconut milk, be sure the flame is not too high.

Yellow Rice Javanese style, with garnishes: Chicken in Mild Sauce (*Opor ayam*); Nut Crackers (*Emping*)

When the boiling point is almost reached, reduce the heat to medium and let it bubble gently. Then the sauce will be smooth and creamy. Stir with down-up-over motion as it comes to the boil and continue stirring for at least ten minutes afterwards to prevent it from curdling. Indonesians use the word 'break' to describe this separation of the coconut milk from its water content. When this happens, the flavour of the spices does not blend with the coconut milk, and the dish tastes flat. But if it does curdle or 'break', do not panic. Just add another cup of thick coconut milk and continue cooking, while stirring gently. This will put it right.

My Australian friends often say: 'You remember the recipe you gave me? I have tried it, but it didn't turn out like yours.' I think this has something to do with the handling of the coconut milk. However, if you follow the preceding directions carefully, you should always get a smooth, delightfully tasting sauce.

NOTE: 1   Never put a lid on while cooking with coconut milk. The only exception to this general rule is when thin coconut milk (type II) is used to parboil tough meat or vegetables. But when the parboiling is finished and the thicker milk has been added, the general rule applies. DO NOT COVER.

2   And even when the dish is finished cooking, while it is still hot, DO NOT COVER.

3   If you are preparing a dish for the following day, using coconut milk, once it has cooled it is best to keep it overnight in the refrigerator to avoid its turning sour. BE SURE TO COVER.

Vegetables cut for Stir-fried Mixed Vegetables with Chicken and Prawns (*Cap chay goreng*)

2 Rice

To MOST Indonesians rice occupies a place similar to that of bread or potatoes in most European diets. Being the staple food and thus the basis of every meal, its cooking has been developed to a fine art; whether it is plain, boiled or prepared as part of an elaborate dish, it must always be cooked to perfection.

Many different varieties of rice are used: white and brown, long and short grain, newly harvested and old rice, highly polished and unpolished. Each type needs slightly different cooking treatment so that, even when following the methods given in this book, a little experimenting is necessary to get satisfactory results, which will depend on the type of rice used and, of course, your personal taste. Some people like their rice soft, others prefer it firm, but certainly no one can enjoy eating it underdone, with granules left in the grain.

The kind of rice to use is a matter of individual preference. Long grain rice is more absorbent and requires a correspondingly greater amount of water in which to cook it than oval grain rice. When cooked, long grain rice is the firmer and dryer; oval grain is the softer and moister. Some people combine the two varieties in the proportions three parts long grain to one part oval grain to get a better flavour and texture.

For entertaining and savoury rice dishes I generally prefer to use the long grain. It has a delicate aroma and the fine slim grains add to the visual appeal of the dish when served.

Plain rice is prepared by steaming or boiling. The former is especially popular, and the manner varies from island to island. In Bali this is traditionally done in a steamer consisting of an earthenware pot and a bamboo steaming basket with the earthenware cover. The grain is rinsed in a bamboo basket to remove the excess starch. The secret of really fluffy rice is in the washing. The rice is then put into an earthen pot of boiling water and left to cook for five minutes. It is then poured into the bamboo steamer which is set into the earthenware pot; the lid is placed over it, and it is steamed for about twenty minutes. From time to time a ladle of boiling water is poured over the rice to prevent it from drying out or the grains sticking together.

The rice is cooked when a grain rubbed between thumb and forefinger has no hard core.

The absorption method is also very common and this method is the easiest to use in this country. The only problem is the amount of water to use. If you ask Indonesians how much water is necessary, you will probably get the answer: 'Enough for the surface of the water to be about a knuckle length of the index finger above the rice in the saucepan.' It may sound a bit quaint, but it is a good guide. An equally effective guide is to allow $1\frac{1}{2}$ cups water to every cup of raw long grain rice, and 1 cup of water to each cup of raw oval rice.

Boiled Rice (Nasi)

ABSORPTION METHOD I

Rinse the rice to remove the excess starch, then spread evenly in a heavy-bottomed saucepan large enough to allow the rice to swell. Add the appropriate quantity of cold water for each cup of rice. Put the lid on the saucepan and bring to boil. Let boil for 1 minute and reduce the heat to medium. Gently stir the rice with the clean handle of a wooden spoon (this will not break the grain) in a circular motion so that the water will be evenly absorbed and the bottom part will not burn. If some rice sticks to the sides of the pan during this stirring, just scrape it down. Cover the saucepan, reduce the heat to very low and let the rice cook another 15-20 minutes until each grain of the rice is tender. Do not lift the lid during the final stage of cooking, otherwise valuable steam will be lost and the rice will be underdone.

Turn off the heat and remove the saucepan from the stove (with the lid still on) and place it on a wet cloth for about 10 minutes. This will prevent the rice from sticking to the bottom of the pan. A crust may form at the bottom of the pan, known as *kerak*. Any such hard crusts can be dried out in the sun, then broken into biscuit-sized pieces and fried until golden brown; salt and eat as a snack.

Goreng kerak, fried rice crust, is crunchy and tasty and can be served as a cracker, like an hors d'oeuvre (crusts from glutinous rice can be prepared in the same manner).

However, the simplest and ideal way for busy wives is to invest in an automatic rice-cooker. There are several good Japanese models in all sizes readily available in large electrical stores.

Boiled Rice (Nasi)

ABSORPTION METHOD II

2 cups oval grain rice   2 cups water

Rinse rice in cold water to remove excess starch. Drain well. Pour the water into a medium saucepan and bring to the boil. Add the rice; spread evenly; cover and allow water to return to the boil. Stir very briefly with the clean handle of a wooden spoon in a circular motion. Cover with well-fitting lid, turn heat as low as possible and let steam for 20 minutes. Fluff up with fork.

Serves 4.

Yellow Rice, Javanese Style (Nasi kuning)

2 cups rice	1 teaspoon turmeric
2½ cups thin coconut milk	1 chicken cube
(or 1½ cups milk and 1 cup water)	2 tablespoons butter

Place rice and ingredients in a saucepan with liquid as mentioned above and cook in the same way as the rice in the previous recipe. The rice has to be turned over several times if cooked with milk, because milk sticks to the bottom of the saucepan. Serve hot on a large serving dish and garnish decoratively with finely sliced omelettes, fried onion flakes, sliced Cucumber and *Abon* (p. 106).

Serves 4.

Creamed Rice (Nasi gurih)

3 cups oval grain rice	½ teaspoon salt
4 cups coconut milk	2 onions, made into fried
2 salam leaves (if available)	onion flakes (p. 107)

Rinse rice in cold water to remove excess starch. Drain well. Pour the coconut milk into a medium saucepan. Add salam leaves and salt and bring to the boil without the lid on, stirring all the time. Add the rice, stir very briefly with the clean handle of a wooden spoon. Cover with well-fitting lid and return to the boil. Allow to boil for 30 seconds. Stir again in circular motion and cover before you turn the heat to very low, and let cook for 20 minutes. Fluff up with a fork. Serve hot and sprinkle onion flakes on top of rice.

This is served for festival occasions together with traditional dishes, such as Spread-eagled Spiced Chicken (p. 96), Meat Potato Croquettes (p. 108), Roasted Coconut with Peanuts (p. 109), Stir-fried Green Beans in Coconut Milk (p. 38).

Serves 4-5.

Simple Fried Rice (Nasi goreng)

1 onion, chopped
1 clove garlic
½ teaspoon shrimp paste
2 tablespoons oil, margarine or butter
2 fresh red chillies, thinly sliced diagonally; discard seeds

2 plates cooked rice
1 tablespoon soya sauce
Salt, to taste
½ cucumber, thinly sliced
1 tomato, cut into thin wedges
2 eggs, lightly fried, yolk should be moist (goreng mata sapi)

Grind onion, garlic and shrimp paste together finely. Heat oil, margarine or butter in a frying pan and stir-fry onion mixture and sliced chillies until fragrant for about 30 seconds. Put in the rice, soya sauce and salt to taste and mix everything thoroughly until the rice grains are well coated and heated through. If the mixture appears too dry, add a little more of the particular fat you happen to be using. Check seasoning. Serve hot on individual plates with peeled thinly-sliced cucumber, tomato wedges arranged decoratively on top of rice with a fried egg in the middle.

Serves 2.

This simple form of fried rice is a typical breakfast dish. From the Indonesian housewives' point of view it is easy to prepare, since the rice is often a leftover from the previous evening's meal. Now, however, it has grown into a dish in its own right with quite elaborate additions and garnishes which has become popular whether for lunch or dinner (see below).

Fried Rice de Luxe (Nasi goreng istimewa)

4 tablespoons margarine or butter
2 cloves garlic
2 onions
250 g (½ pound) fillet steak
Salt
3 cabbage leaves (optional)
4 shallots
2 red peppers or 2 chillies
1 cup bean sprouts

750 g (1½ pounds) rice, steamed or boiled
Thin omelettes (p. 110)
2 tablespoons soya sauce
½ teaspoon monosodium glutamate
250 g (8 ounces) prawns, shelled, deveined and fried briefly in butter
1 small cucumber

Melt margarine or butter, stir-fry crushed garlic and chopped onions for 1 minute. Add steak, sliced into thin strips. Season with salt and cook, stirring continually until meat is tender. Add very thinly sliced cabbage, shallots cut into 2.5 cm (1-inch) pieces, thinly sliced peppers or chillies. Stir continuously. When well mixed, add bean sprouts, then rice, half the omelettes (sliced in fairly thin strips, see below); add soya sauce and monosodium glutamate. Stir in shelled prawns, which have been sautéed in a little butter and seasoned to taste. If mixture appears too dry, add a little more margarine or butter. Taste for seasoning. Serve hot on platter with peeled, thinly-sliced cucumber arranged decoratively around edges. Scatter remaining omelette strips on top of rice. Prepare prawn crackers (p. 104) as a side-dish.

Serves 4.

THIN OMELETTES FOR GARNISH
Beat 3 eggs lightly with 3 tablespoons milk or the same amount of water. Season with salt and pepper to taste. Brush frying pan with margarine; when hot, pour in enough egg mixture to make 1 very thin omelette. Tip pan sideways to thin out omelette. When cooked, roll and slice in fairly thin strips. Repeat process with remaining egg mixture.

Boiled Glutinous Rice (Ketan)

2 cups glutinous rice	Garnish: 1 cup freshly grated
3 cups water	coconut seasoned with salt,
Pinch of salt	to taste

Rinse rice in cold water. Cover rice with water and soak for 1 hour. Drain well. Pour the 3 cups of water into a saucepan and bring to the boil. Add the 2 cups rice. Spread rice evenly wtih a wooden spoon or by shaking the pan gently. Cover and allow water to return to the boil. Stir very briefly with the clean handle of a wooden spoon in a circular motion. Leave to bubble for 60 seconds to let rice absorb most of the water. Cover with well-fitting lid, turn heat as low as possible and let cook for 20 minutes. Serve hot, sprinkled on top with seasoned fresh coconut and accompanied by hot fried bananas.

Serves 6.

Glutinous rice (ketan), as the name implies, is sticky. Farmers—in Central Sumatra anyway—often have it for a morning snack when working in the fields. The womenfolk take it out mid-mornings neatly arranged and balanced on their heads with other sweetmeats. Eaten in quantities, it is heavy on the stomach until one is used to it. If you drop in on friends unexpectedly in rural areas, you're likely to be served boiled glutinous rice together with fried bananas or other home-made and home-grown sweetmeats. This is quickly prepared, meets the requirements of hospitality for a short visit and provides the traveller with something substantial to keep him going until he reaches his destination.

Creamed Glutinous Rice (Nasi lamak)

2 cups glutinous rice	1 pinch of salt
2 cups glutinous rice	

Rinse rice in cold water. Cover rice with water and soak for 1 hour. Drain rice. Pour the coconut milk into a saucepan. Add salt, bring to the boil without the lid on, stirring all the time. Add the rice, stir very briefly with the clean handle of a wooden spoon. Cover with well-fitting lid and return to the boil. Allow to boil for 30 seconds. Stir again in circular motion with the handle of a wooden spoon and cover before you turn the heat to very low, and let cook for 15-20 minutes. Fluff up with a fork. Serve hot.

Serves 4.

This is served for festival occasions together with sweets, such as *Sanok* (p. 138) or Steamed Coconut Custard (*Serikaja*, p. 134).

Festive Yellow Rice (Nasi kunyit)

3 cups glutinous rice	1 pinch of salt
¼ teaspoon turmeric	4 cups coconut milk

Wash rice in several changes of cold water, cover with water. Add turmeric and soak for 3 hours. Drain rice. Cook in coconut milk, seasoned with salt as in the previous recipe.

This turmeric rice is not merely a food, but has a ritual significance. According to custom, it should be accompanied by *Singgang Ayam*, Grilled Spiced Chicken. These two dishes are essential at wedding feasts and are taken as offerings to the grave of a great religious teacher.

As far as I know these are typical Minangkabau dishes. Of course, the rice is delicious when eaten with *Rendang* (p. 81) and *Dendeng Ragi* (p. 77).

Serves 4-5.

Lamb Rice Dish (Nasi kebuli)

6 lamb chump chops
1 piece ginger, 2 inches long
4 cloves garlic
2 onions, sliced
4 tablespoons ghee or oil
1 tablespoon coriander
¼ teaspoon turmeric
Seeds of 2 cardamom pods

1 5 cm (2-inch) cinnamon stick
1 stalk lemon grass
Pepper and salt, to taste
4 cups hot water
Juice of half a lemon
3 cups rice
1 cup sultanas
125 g (¼ pound) almonds, roasted

Trim outer skin of chops, cut into halves, bone and all. Grind ginger, garlic and the sliced onions to a paste. Sauté paste in hot ghee. Add meat, coriander, turmeric, cardamom pods, cinnamon stick, lemon grass, salt and pepper to taste, stirring continuously. When the meat is brown, add hot water and cook the mixture over a moderate heat until the meat is tender. Add lemon juice and check seasoning. Take out meat and put aside and strain the broth. Cook the rice in this strained broth in the usual way. When the rice is almost cooked, add sultanas, give a final stir, then place the meat on top; put the lid on tightly and continue cooking over a low flame until the rice is done (about 15 minutes). Serve on a platter, put the meat pieces in the centre and spoon the rice around it to form a border. Garnish rice with roasted almonds and sprinkle onion flakes on the meat.

Serves 5 or more.

Rice Porridge

Porridge is prepared by simmering a small quantity of rice in a quantity of water, broth or coconut milk until a smooth creamy pulp is formed. It can be made thick or thin depending on the proportion of liquid to rice. If it becomes too thick during cooking, just add more of the particular liquid you are cooking it in.

It is eaten for breakfast or any other time of the day as a snack, and is very popular in mountain areas where the weather can be cold, because it is always served piping hot. Sometimes it is prepared for the sick or elderly, because it is easily digested; prepared plain or cooked with additional ingredients, the bland flavour of the rice allows this porridge to go with just about any kind of meat, poultry or fish.

Rice Porridge with Chicken (Bubur ajam)

Tender 1 kg (2-pound) chicken, cleaned, whole
1 5 cm (2-inch) piece green ginger, scraped and sliced
2 stalks shallots, chopped, green and all
8 cups water
Salt and pepper, to taste
2 tablespoons soya sauce
$\frac{1}{2}$ teaspoon ve-tsin
1 cup raw rice
Parsley, chopped or snipped celeriac top

Place chicken, sliced ginger and chopped shallots in a saucepan with the water. Bring to boil and then simmer with the lid on for about 15 minutes. Add salt, pepper to taste, soya sauce and ve-tsin and simmer for another 45 minutes or until chicken is tender. Check seasoning. Take out chicken, put aside to be cut up into very small pieces. Discard the bones. Strain the chicken broth and cook rice in it to make porridge, substituting broth for water, for about 2 hours. Stir occasionally to prevent rice from sticking to the bottom of the pan and burning. When the porridge is done, add the chicken pieces and reheat through. Garnish with chopped parsley and season with a few drops of soya sauce before serving.

Serves 6.

Compressed Boiled Rice I (Lontong)

Lontong is rice cooked in banana leaves (folded in sausage shape) in boiling water for 2 or 3 hours. It is served instead of boiled rice with certain dishes, and is also very practical for informal parties for it is eaten cold (room temperature) and usually prepared a day before, so that it will become firm. It will keep three days without refrigeration.

Where banana leaves cannot be obtained, substitute cheese cloth bags about 15 cm (6 inches) long and 3.5 cm (1½ inches) in diameter.

Fill bags about two-thirds full with washed oval grain rice and cook in boiling water for 2-3 hours. The idea of cooking rice this way, is to make the grains swell to capacity in a limited space, so that the rice will become a firm lump. Fifteen minutes before removing from water, add a few drops of green food colouring. This gives the outer part a soft green colour, and suggests that it has been cooked in banana leaves. Remove *Lontong* from bags only when it is time to serve it. Cut into 1.5 cm (½-inch) slices. Serve it with the following set of dishes: *Opor ayam* (p. 92), *Sambal goreng buncis* (p. 38) and *Serundeng* (p. 109). It is also often served with charcoal-grilled meat on skewers *(Satés)* with peanut butter sauce. Very popular in Indonesian restaurants, served as snacks after the cinema or as a weekend treat—a boy often takes his girlfriend to a restaurant for some *Lontong*.

Compressed Boiled Rice II (Ketupat)

Another form of compressed boiled rice is prepared by cooking it in small square bags (other shapes are also possible) woven from young coconut palm leaves; this way is similar to that of preparing *Lontong,* e.g. by filling each bag three-quarters full and boiling for 2 or 3 hours. Glutinous rice is also cooked in the *Ketupat* manner, boiled in coconut milk instead of water and served as part of a sweet dish; another interesting way of cooking compressed glutinous rice with thick coconut milk is in a hollow bamboo, which has been lined with young banana leaves, and is then set around a big open fire to cook. It is also served as part of a sweet and sometimes is eaten with *Rendang* or *Dendeng ragi*.

3 Vegetables

In a country such as Australia we take the availability of a wide range of fruit and vegetables, either fresh or frozen, for granted. Since Australia is a continent which extends over several climatic zones, fresh fruit and vegetables of one kind or another are available all through the year, including some which are familiar in Indonesia, and transport is no problem. To these can be added many produced in other parts of the world, dried, frozen or in tins. Such a variety is a constant challenge to the aspiring cook, for the freshness and colour of these vegetables, when displayed in an open-air market, is both appetising and compelling.

In Indonesia on the other hand, it is only in certain areas, where the soil is fertile and well irrigated, particularly the cooler hilly regions, that vegetables flourish in varieties even more numerous than those generally known in temperate zones. Unfortunately, no efficient nationwide system of distribution and marketing yet exists, and the processes of canning and freezing are virtually unknown.

Nevertheless, a vegetable dish can require as much care as the preparation of meat, poultry or fish. It may even serve as the main dish. *Pecel* (p. 42), or *Gado-gado padang* (p. 41) accompanied by *Rempeyek* (p. 105) or *Krupuk* (p. 104), make an agreeably substantial meal.

The preparation and cooking of vegetables is an art in itself, a fact my grandmother did her best to bring home to me. They have to be cut properly, and different ways of cooking require different styles of cutting. Some vegetables, such as young bean sprouts, baby green beans, heart of cabbage and young aubergines, are served raw (p. 42). Others may be steamed accompanied by one of the many varieties of sambal, stir-fried or boiled. But whatever technique is used, vegetables are not overcooked; thus they are served slightly crisp, still retaining a fresh colour.

Steaming in a bamboo steamer is a time-honoured method still popular among peasants and country people. If more than one kind is to be cooked, the vegetables are put into it in order of cooking times required, those requiring the longest time being put in first, those requiring the least, last. To save work, young tender vegetables may be steamed on top of the rice during the last stage of cooking. Only a small quantity can be cooked in this way, however, otherwise too much steam will be absorbed, and the rice be undercooked, but certainly enough can be cooked in this way for one or two persons.

Boiling is a way of cooking that contains several dangers. It is important not to cook for too long or to use too much water. Some vegetables, such as spinach, have a high water content—this needs only the water clinging to its leaves after washing. Otherwise, sufficient boiling water to cover the vegetables is necessary, together with 1 chilli (whole), 1 onion (chopped) and salt to taste. Vegetables are boiled in a covered saucepan. The cooking time depends on the texture of the vegetables, whether tough or tender. But the general rule must be strictly followed: do not overcook.

The stir-fry method is very popular because it makes a very tasty dish. The vegetables need to be cut into small pieces both for easy stirring and even cooking. The stir-frying is done in oil or margarine with onion, salt, pepper (or chillies) and other ingredients. A little water or coconut milk is added to moisten the vegetables. Boiling water is better than cold water for this purpose. The cooking time is shortened and the fresh colour preserved.

Boiled Cabbage (Rebus kol)

1 green cabbage, about 1 kg (2 pounds)	Salt
	Water, to cover cabbage
1 onion, quartered	
1 fresh chilli, whole	

Remove and discard discoloured outer leaves from green cabbage. Wash and cut cabbage into 6 or 8 wedges. Secure each wedge with a thin bamboo skewer to keep the leaves together. Place cabbage wedges, quartered onion and chilli into saucepan of boiling salted water. Boil for 15 minutes or 20 minutes. Drain and remove skewers. Arrange on a serving dish.

Serves 8.

Cabbage Cooked in Coconut Milk (Gulai manis kol)

1 small green cabbage, 750 g
  (1½ pounds)
4 cups coconut milk
2 onions, thinly sliced
2 fresh red chillies, whole
½ teaspoon laos

5 cm (2-inch) piece green ginger
  scraped and sliced
2 salam leaves (if available)
½ teaspoon ve-tsin
Salt, to taste

Cut cabbage in quarters, remove hard cores, and cut it into 4 cm (1½-inch) pieces. Place coconut milk in a saucepan with all the other ingredients and salt to taste. Bring to boil, stirring continuously with down-up-over motion. Add prepared cabbage as soon as the coconut milk comes to boil and continue cooking until cabbage is tender for about 10 or 15 minutes. Do not overcook.

Serves 6.

The same recipe can be prepared using almost any vegetables.

Stir-fried Cabbage and Eggs (Orak arik)

1 large onion, finely sliced
1 red chilli, thinly, diagonally
  sliced; discard seeds
1 tablespoon butter or margarine
1 chicken cube

250 g (½ pound) cabbage, finely
  shredded
Salt, to taste
2 eggs

Sauté sliced onion and chilli in butter until they change colour. Break up chicken cube and add shredded cabbage and salt, to taste, to onion mixture; stir it thoroughly. Cook for about 10 minutes with lid on. Before serving add beaten eggs. Stir in well. Serve hot, sprinkled with onion flakes on top.

Serves 4.

Stuffed Cabbage in Broth (Kol isi berkuah)

10 (or more) Savoy cabbage leaves

STUFFING

1 small onion, thinly sliced
3 cloves garlic, finely chopped
2 tablespoons margarine or butter
500 g (1 pound) minced steak
Salt and pepper, to taste
¼ teaspoon nutmeg

3 shallots, thinly sliced, including
  green tops
2 pieces of bread soaked in
  ¼ cup milk
2 eggs

BROTH

1 onion, finely sliced
2 cloves garlic, finely chopped
2 tablespoons margarine,
  or butter
1 cup water
2 tablespoons soya sauce

1 beef cube
¼ teaspoon nutmeg
8 black peppercorns, whole
Salt, to taste
30 g (1 ounce) shiny type vermicelli
  soaked in hot water

To prepare the stuffing: stir-fry sliced onions and garlic in butter until they change colour, then add meat seasoned with salt, pepper and nutmeg, stirring constantly. When meat is half-cooked, add sliced shallots. Remove from heat as soon as meat is cooked. In bowl combine meat mixture thoroughly with 2 eggs and bread pulp. Correct seasoning. Blanch cabbage leaves in boiling water for 5 minutes. Drain well. On each cabbage leaf put 1 dessertspoonful of stuffing, roll up the leaves like small parcels, tucking or folding in the ends. Arrange in a heatproof casserole and put temporary weight on them so that they remain firmly rolled up, or secure with toothpicks. For this dish I prefer to use Savoy cabbage because of its tender leaves, which are curly, deep green in colour and more delicate in flavour than white cabbage.

To prepare the broth: sauté sliced onions and garlic in butter until brown. Add water, soya sauce, beef cube, nutmeg and black peppercorns. Season with salt to taste. Bring to boil. Pour broth into the casserole on stuffed cabbages. Cover and cook for about 20 minutes. Add vermicelli 5 minutes before serving.

Serves 5.

Stir-fried Chinese Cabbage and Dried Shrimp (Tumis sawi dengan udang kering)

5 dried shrimps
500 g (1 pound) Chinese cabbage
2 onions, thinly sliced
1 clove garlic, chopped

Salt, to taste
2 tablespoons oil or margarine
1 capsicum, sliced in strips,
  discard seeds

Soak dried shrimps in hot water for half an hour or until soft. Cut up into titbits. Cut cabbage stems in 5 cm (2-inch) sections. Stir-fry onion and garlic with salt in hot oil lightly. Add soaked shrimp titbits and cook for 3 minutes. Add cabbage, capsicum strips and stir-fry for 5-7 minutes until cabbage is cooked. Serve hot.

Serves 4.

Stir-fried Snow Peas (*Tumis arcis*)

500 g (1 pound) snow peas
1 onion, thinly sliced
2 tablespoons margarine
1 tablespoon soya sauce

¼ cup boiling water
¼ teaspoon monosodium glutamate
  (optional)
Salt, to taste

Wash, top and tail peas. Fry sliced onion in melted margarine until slices change colour. Add snow peas, soya sauce, water, (monosodium glutamate) and salt to taste. Stir-fry for 5 minutes.

Serves 4.

Spinach

To cook, discard any wilted or yellow leaves, plunge into a large basin of cold water and pump it up and down for several minutes with your hands. Lift it out into a colander, leaving any soil in the bottom of the basin. If necessary, wash spinach a few times more until there is no soil to be seen in the bottom of the basin. Drain; if the spinach is young and tender, cut into 5 cm (2-inch) lengths, stems and all. Separate stems and leaves if it is older, for stems require longer cooking than leaves.

Stir-fried Spinach (*Tumis bayam*)

500 g (1 pound) bunch spinach
1 medium onion, sliced
Salt, to taste
1 red chilli, diagonally sliced,
  discard seeds

½ teaspoon shrimp paste
  (optional)
2 tablespoons oil or margarine
1 cup hot water or stock

Prepare and wash the spinach as described above. Stir-fry onions with salt, chilli and shrimp paste in hot oil until they are golden. Add the prepared spinach. Stir-fry to soften lightly. Stir in water or stock. Serve when this is really hot.

Serves 2.

Spinach and Sweet Corn (Sayur menir)

500 g (1 pound) bunch spinach
3 ears sweet corn (or 1 small tin
   whole kernel, drained)
2 small onions, sliced

1 clove garlic, crushed
½ teaspoon shrimp paste
2 cups stock
Salt, to taste

Slice the corn from the cob (or open the tin) and boil it in the stock with the other ingredients except the spinach until corn is tender. Add the prepared spinach stems first; boil for 2 minutes, then add the leaves and cook for another 4-5 minutes or until spinach is tender.

Serves 4.

Stir-fried Silver Beet (Tumis bayam silver bit)

2 tablespoons margarine
1 small onion
1 bunch silver beet or spinach
1 green capsicum

6-8 shallots
Salt, to taste
1 cup hot water or stock

Melt margarine in frying pan, fry thinly sliced onion. When it changes colour add silver beet, which has been washed and cut into even pieces, the capsicum, cut into rings, shallots, cut into 5 cm (2-inch) pieces including green tops; season with salt. Keep turning vegetables so they cook evenly. When vegetables begin to shrink, add water or stock. Cover, bring to boil; remove cover, turn vegetables again. Taste silver beet; if cooked, remove from heat at once. Be careful not to overcook vegetables.

Serves 4.

Sauteed Zucchini (Tumis oyong)

6 zucchini
1 onion, thinly sliced
1 chilli, thinly diagonally sliced
2 tablespoons margarine or butter

Salt, to taste
½ cup hot water
30 g (1 ounce) shiny type vermicelli,
   soaked in hot water

Cut unpeeled zucchini into slices, 2.5 cm (1-inch) thick. Stir-fry sliced onions and chilli until golden in margarine. Add zucchini and sauté for 5 minutes, stirring frequently. Add to the onion/zucchini mixture ½ cup

Stir-fried Mixed Vegetables with Chicken and Prawns (Cap chay goreng)

hot water and season to taste with salt. Make sure the water is very hot. Just before serving, stir in vermicelli and sprinkle with onion flakes.

Serves 4.

Sautéed Bean Sprouts (Tumis tauge)

2 tablespoons margarine or oil
1 small onion, sliced
6 shallots
Salt and pepper, to taste

¼ cup hot water
¼ teaspoon monosodium
    glutamate (optional)
500 g (1 pound) bean sprouts

Melt margarine or oil, fry sliced onion. When it changes colour, add shallots cut into 5 cm (2-inch) lengths, salt, pepper to taste, and hot water. Bring to boil, add monosodium glutamate; add cleaned, washed bean sprouts; stir. Cook another 3 minutes. Remove from heat and serve.

Serves 6.

Stir-fried Mixed Vegetables with Chicken and Prawns (Cap chay goreng)

1 quarter cauliflower
250 g (½ pound) carrots
250 g (½ pound) fresh peas
125 g (¼ pound) mushrooms
2 sprigs celeriac top
1 chicken breast
250 g (8 ounces) medium-sized
    prawns
3 tablespoons oil
1 onion, thinly sliced

3 cloves garlic, chopped
3 slices green ginger
Salt, to taste
½ teaspoon cornflour
2 chicken stock cubes, dissolved
    in 1 cup hot water
2 teaspoons soya sauce
Freshly ground pepper
¼ teaspoon monosodium glutamate
    (optional)

Break cauliflower into small flowerets and parboil. Peel carrots. Run points of fork down carrots all around. Then slice very thinly and parboil. Shell peas; slice mushrooms through cap and stem; break celeriac up into small sections; skin, bone and slice chicken into thin strips; shell and devein prawns. Have all ingredients ready near the stove. Heat oil, add onion, garlic, ginger and salt and stir-fry until soft. Do not brown onion. Add chicken strips and cook until they change colour. Add prawns and stir-fry until they turn pink. Add peas, mushrooms, cauliflower, carrots, celeriac top, in that order and stir-fry. Add cornflour

Vegetable Salad with Peanut
Sauce (Gado-gado)

which has been mixed with chicken stock, soya sauce, pepper, mono-sodium glutamate. Bring to boil and turn a few times. Check the doneness of vegetables and seasonings. The vegetables should be cooked but crisp.

Serves 6.

This is a dish which any hostess would be proud to serve, as much for visual appeal as for taste.

Tangy Vegetable Dish (Sayur asam Jawa)

2 cloves garlic
1 onion
½ teaspoon shrimp paste, slightly grilled
4 macadamia nuts
2 chillies
2 salam leaves
3 cups beef stock
1 tablespoon tamarind juice
Salt, to taste

½ cup peanuts, washed
125 g (¼ pound) green beans, cut into 2.5 cm (1-inch) pieces
1 large eggplant, cut into cubes
2 large green tomatoes, cut into cubes
5 cabbage leaves, hard cores removed, cut into 5 cm (2-inch) squares ·

Pound chillies, garlic, onion, shrimp paste and macadamia nuts into a smooth paste. Place beef stock, paste, salam leaves and tamarind juice with salt to taste in a saucepan. Bring to boil, add peanuts and cook for 2 minutes. Then add beans, followed by eggplant, tomato cubes and cook till tender. Add cabbage pieces 2 minutes before cooking is completed. To serve, place vegetables and stock in a large serving bowl.

Serves 4.

Many Westerners refer to this and similar dishes as soups. As I have mentioned several times, this is not how Indonesians see it. To them it is just a vegetable dish with a tasty sauce that contributes to the flavour of the rice to which it is added.

Crunchy Cucumber Relish (Acar ketimun)

5 fresh cucumbers
1 tablespoon salt
5 candlenuts (or 5 macadamia nuts)
3 cloves garlic
½ teaspoon turmeric
5 cm (2-inch) piece green ginger

2 tablespoons oil
2 onions, quartered
2 fresh chillies, whole and scraped
Salt, to taste
1 teaspoon sugar
¼ cup vinegar
¼ cup water

Peel cucumbers and cut lengthwise into quarters; discard the pulpy centres with seeds. Cut uniformly into fingers. Season heavily with 1 tablespoon salt. Place in the refrigerator for 1 hour. Rinse the cucumber with cold water and drain well. Wrap in a teatowel to remove excess moisture. Place nuts, garlic, turmeric and ginger in a blender and blend with 2 tablespoons water into a smooth paste. Stir-fry the paste in hot oil together with onion, chilli and salt for about 1 minute or until fragrant. Add sugar, vinegar and water. Bring gently to boil, stirring. Add cucumber and mix well. Check seasoning. Leave to cool. Serve at room temperature or chilled, as a side-dish.

Serves 10.

The taste is fresh, nutty, and the cucumber has a good crunch to it. This is excellent served with rich-tasting meat dishes. It also goes well with cold meat. It will keep up to one week in a refrigerator.

Cucumber Salad (Slada mentimun)

2 large green cucumbers	2 tablespoons prepared mayonnaise
1 teaspoon salt	$\frac{1}{4}$ teaspoon mustard
3 hard-boiled eggs	Salt and pepper, to taste

Garnish: tomato slices; 3 or 4 lettuce cups; 60 g (2 ounces) unbroken potato crisps; boiled egg white, sliced into strips; 1 tablespoon fried onion flakes.

Peel cucumbers. Run points of fork down cucumber, all around, then slice. Season with salt. Place in refrigerator for 1 hour. Press lightly and pour off all the liquid that collects. Halve boiled eggs lengthwise. Remove egg yolks, mash and combine with mayonnaise, mustard, salt and pepper. Rub the egg yolk mixture into cucumber slices. Adjust seasoning. Heap cucumber slices on to lettuce-lined shallow bowl, trim with tomato slices, alternating with potato crisps. Scatter boiled egg white strips and fried onion flakes over the top.

Serves 4.

Cucumber Salad, Traditional Style (Acar bening)

1 cucumber	1 fresh red chilli, sliced thinly
$\frac{1}{2}$ teaspoon salt	in rings, discard seeds
1 tablespoon vinegar	1 shallot stalk (the white part),
$\frac{1}{2}$ teaspoon sugar	sliced thinly in rings

Peel and slice cucumber thinly. Sprinkle with salt. Press lightly and drain. Make a dressing with vinegar and sugar. Combine dressing with cucumber slices, chilli and shallot rings and chill until required.

Serves 4.

Green Bean and Bean Sprout Salad (Slada buncis dengan tauge)

250 g (½ pound) green beans
250 g (½ pound) fresh bean sprouts
3 hard-boiled eggs

60 g (2 ounces) potato crips
2 tablespoons fried onion flakes

Top and tail beans, cut in halves, first lengthwise then crosswise; boil and drain. Put aside. Scald cleaned and washed bean sprouts. Drain and put aside.

DRESSING

3 hard-boiled eggs
1 tablespoon butter
¼ teaspoon prepared mustard

1 teaspoon sugar
Salt and pepper, to taste
1 tablespoon vinegar

Halve boiled eggs lengthwise. Remove egg yolks. Cut egg whites into thin strips; put aside for garnish. Cream butter until light. Add mashed egg yolks, mustard, sugar, salt and pepper and mix thoroughly. Add vinegar, stir and check seasoning. Toss the beans and bean sprouts in dressing. Just before serving, arrange potato crisps as a border and vegetables in the centre of a platter. Scatter egg white strips and fried onion flakes on top decoratively. This goes very well with *Bistik* (p. 79).

Serves 4.

Stir-fried Green Beans in Coconut Milk (Sambal goreng buncis)

2 tablespoons oil or margarine
1 onion, thinly sliced
2 cloves garlic, crushed
3 pieces green ginger,
    about 1 cm (½ inch) thick
1-2 fresh chillies, diagonally sliced,
    discard seeds
1 salam leaf (if available)

¼ teaspoon shrimp paste
Salt, to taste
500 g (1 pound) green beans
1 cup coconut milk
¼ teaspoon paprika
4 shallot stalks, cut into
    5 cm (2-inch) lengths

Heat oil or margarine, stir-fry onion, garlic, ginger, chilli, salam leaf and shrimp paste with salt to taste until fragrant (about 60 seconds). Add beans which have been sliced diagonally thinly and evenly. Cook for about 3 minutes, turning beans occasionally. Add coconut milk and paprika, if you wish; stir continually to avoid curdling; bring to boil. Add shallots and keep on stirring. Check seasoning. When the beans are tender, remove from heat. Serve hot. The paprika is for colouring; without it the dish may look anaemic.

Serves 4.

Tomatoes in Coconut Milk (Sambal goreng tomat)

1 tablespoon oil or margarine	2.5 cm (1-inch) piece ginger, sliced
1 onion, thinly sliced	2 salam leaves (if available)
2 cloves garlic, chopped	1 cup coconut milk
2 fresh red chillies, thinly sliced diagonally, discard seeds; or 1 teaspoon ground red chilli	Salt, to taste
	1 teaspoon sugar
	4 medium-firm tomatoes, washed and cut into small wedges
½ teaspoon shrimp paste	

Heat oil and stir-fry onion, garlic, chilli (sliced or ground), shrimp paste, ginger and salam leaves for 1 minute. Add coconut milk, salt to taste and sugar. Bring to boil while stirring. Add tomato wedges and cook for another 3 minutes until tomatoes are wilted but not mushy.

Serves 4.

Mixed Vegetables in Coconut Milk (Sayur lodeh)

1 tablespoon margarine or oil	2 eggplants, cubed
1 onion, thinly sliced	1 small tomato, peeled and diced
2 cloves garlic, sliced	Salt, to taste
½ teaspoon shrimp paste	1½ cups thin coconut milk (style II p. 17)
1 5 cm (2-inch) piece green ginger, sliced	1 cup very thick coconut milk (style I p. 17)
2 salam leaves (if available)	1 teaspoon sugar, optional
1 tablespoon ground coriander	
25 g (½ pound) green beans	
1 choko, peeled and cut uniformly into chunks	

Heat margarine, add sliced onion, sliced garlic, cook until onion slices change colour. Add shrimp paste, sliced ginger, salam leaves and coriander and stir-fry briefly for about 10 seconds. Add beans cut into 4 cm (1½-inch) slices, choko in chunks, cubed eggplant, diced tomato, and salt to taste. Turn over a few times; add thin coconut milk. Bring to boil. Add the thick coconut milk a few minutes before the vegetables are tender. Bring back to boil, stirring to prevent coconut milk from curdling. Add (if desired) sugar and check seasoning. As soon as the mixture comes to the boil, the vegetables should be tender. Serve hot.

Serves 4-5.

Mixed Vegetable Relish (Acar kuning)

6 macadamia nuts or candlenuts
500 g (1 pound) green beans
500 g (1 pound) carrots
6-8 shallots or 4 small white
   onions
1 onion
3 tablespoons margarine or oil
2 cloves garlic

½ teaspoon turmeric
¼ cup vinegar
Salt, to taste
1 teaspoon sugar
2 chicken stock cubes
2 cups hot water
3 red chillies (whole, scrape
   stems) or 2 red capsicums

Prepare vegetables and nuts. Grind nuts finely in a mincer, set aside. Choose young, small green beans. Top and tail them, cut in halves, first lengthwise, then crosswise. Scrape carrots, cut into matchstick-sized strips. Cut shallots into 5 cm (2-inch) lengths, or peel and quarter white onions. Thinly slice onion, fry in melted margarine until slices change colour; reduce heat. Add ground macadamia nuts, crushed garlic, turmeric. Cook, stirring constantly, about 1 minute. Add prepared vegetables, vinegar, salt, sugar, and stock (made by dissolving stock cubes in hot water). Bring to boil, stirring. Reduce heat, cook until vegetables are tender (test by tasting beans; they should taste cooked but be crisp and crunchy—the result of adding the vegetables and vinegar at the same time). Turn into serving dish.

This is an excellent accompaniment to rich-tasting dishes such as meat and chicken dishes with coconut milk; it also goes well with cold meats. Covered, it will keep up to one week in the refrigerator.

Padang Vegetable Salad with Peanut Sauce (Gado-gado Padang)

½ fresh green cabbage, white
    and green separated
1 small cucumber
3 medium-sized potatoes,
    boiled in jackets

3 hard-boiled eggs
A few slices of braised beef in soya
    sauce to add flavour (p. 79)
¼ cup fried onion flakes
Krupuk

Slice the green cabbage leaves finely and scald. Slice finely the raw white cabbage leaves, chill in refrigerator. Wash cucumber, run points of fork down cucumber all around. Then slice thinly. Arrange salad on a serving plate; the green sliced cabbage as border and the white cabbage in the centre. Arrange the remaining vegetables and eggs decoratively on top. Pour over the sauce (see below); garnish with slices of braised beef in soya sauce (p. 79), fried onion flakes (p. 107) and crackers or *Krupuk* (p. 104).

Serves 6.

PEANUT SAUCE

1 cup raw peanuts
1 large onion, thinly sliced
2 cloves garlic, thinly sliced
1 teaspoon ground chilli
1 lemon leaf (optional)
½ teaspoon shrimp paste

1 cup oil
2 cups coconut milk or water
1 teaspoon brown sugar
½ teaspoon grated lemon rind
1 tablespoon vinegar
Salt, to taste

Fry the peanuts until cooked and let cool. Rub off the inner skins and discard. Pound or vitamise peanuts until they form a fine paste. Stir-fry onion, garlic, chilli, lemon leaf and shrimp paste in 2 tablespoons hot oil until fragrant. Add coconut milk (or water) and ground peanuts, stirring constantly until the mixture comes to the boil. Add sugar, lemon rind, vinegar and salt to taste; let simmer until it thickens. Check seasoning. Serve at room temperature. If too thick, add a little hot water.

Place a small bowl of Chilli Sauce on the table also for diners to help themselves (see following recipe).

CHILLI SAUCE (optional)

2 teaspoons finely ground chilli
Salt, to taste

Juice of half a lemon or
1 tablespoon vinegar
2 tablespoons oil

Fry chilli in hot oil on low heat. Season with salt and lemon or vinegar. Place in a small dish.

Salad with Peanut Sauce (Gado-gado)

3 medium potatoes
225 g (½ pound) green beans
2-3 carrots
¼ cabbage

1 lettuce
2 medium tomatoes
3-4 hard-boiled eggs
1 tablespoon crisp fried onion flakes

Boil potatoes in their jackets; skin and dice. Cut beans into thin, diagonal slices; boil and drain. Scrape carrots, cut into matchstick-sized strips; boil and drain. Shred cabbage very finely. Put into boiling water, bring to boil again (don't overcook); drain. Arrange vegetables on a platter as follows: first, the washed, well-crisped lettuce around the edges, then potatoes, cabbage, beans, carrots, sliced or quartered tomatoes, sliced or quartered eggs. This gives a nice contrast of colours. Or, place vegetables decoratively in lettuce cups for individual helpings, on a platter. Sprinkle with onion flakes. Pour over the Peanut Sauce just before serving. This goes very well with a grill, or serve it as a barbecue salad. For a quick, tasty salad, pour the sauce over hard-boiled eggs, lettuce, and tomatoes.

Serves 9.

PEANUT SAUCE

1 medium onion
2 tablespoons margarine or oil
1-2 teaspoons ground chilli
2½ cups water
1 cup peanut butter or the same
    quantity of ground roasted
    peanuts

1 teaspoon salt, or to taste
1 tablespoon white vinegar
1 teaspoon sugar

Sauté chopped onion in margarine until transparent. Add ground chilli, reduce heat; add water, then peanut butter and cook for a few minutes, stirring constantly. Bring to boil on a medium heat. Continue stirring until mixture becomes smooth. Season to taste with salt, vinegar, and sugar. This sauce is nice if served hot in winter and at room temperature in summer.

Mixed Vegetable Salad (Pecal)

125 g (¼ pound) green beans, cut
    into 2.5 cm (1-inch) lengths
    and boiled
One ¼ cabbage, shredded and
    scalded
125 g (¼ pound) bamboo shoots,
    thinly sliced and cut into sticks

125 g (¼ pound) bean sprouts,
    scalded
A few prawn crackers
    (Krupuk udang), fried (p. 104)

PEANUT BUTTER SAMBAL

2 *fresh whole chillies*
2 *onions, quartered*
$\frac{1}{4}$ *teaspoon kencur (optional)*
1 *teaspoon brown sugar*
2 *tablespoons tamarind juice*
  (or juice of 1 lemon)
1 *teaspoon grated lemon rind*

1 *small piece shrimp paste,*
  grilled (optional)
1 *cup peanut butter (crunchy*
  type) or the same quantity of
  ground roasted peanuts
Salt, to taste

Stir-fry chilli and onion until soft. Place chilli, onion, *kencur*, sugar, tamarind juice, lemon rind and shrimp paste in a blender and blend with 2 tablespoons water into a smooth paste. Mix together paste with peanut butter and salt to taste. Check seasoning. Put aside until ready to use. Dilute with hot water according to required quantity and consistency.

TO SERVE
Arrange vegetables attractively on a platter and pour the diluted peanut sauce into a bowl. Put prawn crackers *(krupuk)* in a small bamboo basket or on a wooden tray. Each person helps himself to what he likes from the vegetable platter, to as much sauce as he likes and of course, to the crackers, which give crunchy taste to every mouthful.

Serves 6.

Vegetable Salad with Coconut Dressing (Urap)

1 *choko, peeled and cut*
  into matchsticks
250 *g ($\frac{1}{2}$ pound) green beans,*
  topped and tailed, sliced
  diagonally

125 *g ($\frac{1}{4}$ pound) bamboo shoots,*
  cut into matchsticks
125 *g ($\frac{1}{4}$ pound) bean sprouts*

Boil choko, beans and bamboo shoots separately. Scald bean sprouts.

DRESSING
125 *g ($\frac{1}{4}$ pound) desiccated or*
  fresh grated coconut
1 *small onion, grated*
2 *cloves garlic, crushed*
2 *fresh red chillies, finely ground*

$\frac{1}{2}$ *teaspoon prawn paste,*
  lightly grilled
Juice of half a lemon
Salt, to taste

Mix together thoroughly the coconut, spices and salt to taste. Steam until mixture is hot and cooked all through. Let cool. Toss two-thirds of coconut dressing with prepared vegetables, arrange attractively on a platter and spread the remaining dressing on top.

Serves 5.

This is usually served with rice to accompany a fish or meat dish, but is always good eaten by itself.

Eggplant

In Indonesia there is a variety of eggplants. You will find the white eggplant, similar in shape and texture to the more common purple variety, but smaller (about the size of a cucumber), less pulpy and more delicate and sweet. The other type is round like a ball and the size of an apple.

Since eggplant has a high water content, after cutting as required for a recipe, sprinkle with salt, allow to stand for half an hour or so to let the liquid drain away, then dry on absorbent paper.

Steamed Eggplant (Uap terung)

2 eggplants

Cut off stems and wash. Score skin with 4 equidistant lengthwise slashes, about 1 cm ($\frac{1}{2}$-inch) deep. Place in a small heatproof dish. Steam for 15-20 minutes or until tender. This goes very well with Coconut Fish Roe Sambal (*Sambal kelapa dengan telur terubuk*, p. 99).

Serves 4.

I usually steam an eggplant on top of rice during the last stage of cooking, i.e. after giving it a final stir and before replacing the lid (p. 30).

Fried Eggplant (Goreng terung)

2 medium-sized eggplants   *Paprika*
Oil   *Salt*

Wash and dry eggplants, cut into fairly thick slices. Heat oil in frypan, deep-fry eggplant slices, making sure they are covered by oil. Cook until tender and lightly browned; drain. While still hot sprinkle with salt and paprika and with crisp fried onions. This dish can be prepared the day before and refrigerated overnight; drain off any surplus liquid before reheating in moderate oven.

Serves 4.

Curried Eggplant and Beef (Gulai terung dengan daging)

500 g (1 pound) eggplant	*½ teaspoon turmeric*
500 g (1 pound) round steak	*1 5 cm (2-inch) piece ginger,*
Oil	*scraped and sliced*
2 onions, thinly sliced	*1 stalk lemon grass, bruised*
5 fresh chillies, thinly sliced,	*Salt, to taste*
discard seeds or 1 capsicum,	*Juice of half a lemon*
sliced into thin strips	*2 cups coconut milk*

Wash and cut eggplants into 2.5 cm (1-inch) slices. Treat slices as above. Put aside. Cut steak into 2.5 cm (1-inch) cubes. Heat oil in pan, add all ingredients except steak, lemon juice and coconut milk and stir-fry until fragrant for about 3 minutes. Then add steak and cook over high heat, stirring to mix well with the spice mixture. Pour in coconut milk into steak mixture and bring to boil, stirring continuously with up-down-over motion. Adjust seasoning. Reduce heat and let simmer until meat is tender. Add prepared eggplant slices and slowly bring to boil again. Add lemon juice, stir and adjust seasoning. Finish the cooking on low heat until eggplant is tender, for about 8 or 10 minutes. Serve hot.

Serves 6.

Broccoli with Toasted Coconut Dressing (Anyang brokoli)

500 g (1 pound) broccoli	*2 fresh red chillies*
125 g (¼ pound) desiccated coconut	*½ teaspoon shrimp paste,*
or 1 cup freshly grated coconut	*lightly grilled*
1 small onion, quartered	*Salt, to taste*
1 clove garlic	*Juice of half a lemon*

Soak broccoli for a few minutes in salted water and rinse. Trim tough ends and peel stems. Cut and rinse. Cut into pieces of uniform length, about 2 inches. Place stems in the bottom of saucepan. Add 1 inch boiling salted water, cover and cook until stems are just tender, for 10-15 minutes. Drain well. Put aside. Stir grated or desiccated coconut in some hot oil on a low heat together with onion, garlic and chilli until coconut is brown and other ingredients are tender. Grind these ingredients into a fine paste together with shrimp paste and salt to taste. Add lemon juice and mix well. Check seasonings. Coat boiled broccoli with coconut dressing and serve.

Serves 4.

Broccoli Sumatran Style (Brokoli a la gulai pakis)

1 kg (2 pounds) broccoli
1 tablespoon ground chilli
2 onions, quartered
3 cloves garlic
1 5 cm (2-inch) piece green
   ginger
5 macadamia nuts
¼ teaspoon turmeric

4 cups coconut milk
1 stalk lemon grass, bruised
4 basil leaves
½ tin anchovy fillets cut into
   2.5 cm (1-inch) pieces
Salt, to taste

Choose fresh broccoli with green flowerets without any yellow buds. Trim tough ends and peel stems. Cut into pieces of uniform length, about 2 inches. In an electric blender grind together chilli, onion, garlic, ginger, nuts and turmeric with 2 tablespoons water into a smooth paste. Pour coconut milk into a large saucepan. Add nut paste, lemon grass, basil leaves, anchovies and salt to taste. Bring to boil stirring constantly. Leave to cook on moderate heat until the coconut milk thickens and its volumes reduces by about half. Add broccoli and continue cooking, stirring occasionally, for about 15 minutes or until the vegetables are tender. The broccoli will now be coated with a rich creamy sauce. Serve hot.

Serves 8.

In Indonesia, the young tender shoots of a certain type of fern (pakis is the Indonesian word for ferns in general) are cooked in this way. It is a dish of Sumatran origin which has become popular throughout the archipelago. As far as I know, this kind of fern is not available in Australia although it may grow in North Queensland, but broccoli is an ideal substitute.

Grilled Fresh Corn on the Cob (*Jagung panggang*)

Remove husks and silk from fresh corn. Leave stem intact. Place on grill and roast over hot coals 15-20 minutes or until corn is cooked, turning ears frequently. Ideal for barbecues. Listen to them popping and have them piping hot, while burgers broil and steaks sizzle. In Indonesia, corn is often sold at the roadside by hawkers who grill it straight from the field for passers-by. Indonesians are great munchers and this is a popular afternoon snack among young people, whether they are out for a stroll or watching a football match.

4 *Eggs*

EGGS are usually taken for granted, yet have you ever stopped for a moment to think what life would be like without them? Although a simple food, much depends on eggs which are used or treated much the same everywhere in the world. But they have many special advantages in a country like Indonesia where visiting plays such an important part in the life of the community—as a sign of respect, interest, sympathy, gratitude, appreciation and for many other reasons, in addition to the ones common in this country. This institution of visiting is one of the bonds that ensures a sense of community among family kinsfolk and clan. The rhythm of visiting and the sense of obligation on the part of the host is more complex in Indonesia than in a Western country. Communications and distance make the timing of a visit approximate; and in any case it is regarded as imposing, or in fact arrogance, to announce a visit. The corollary to this institution of visiting is hospitality: a guest may have travelled miles without refreshment. And since in the very nature of things guests in general are expected but in particular unexpected, it is eggs which provide the key to instant hospitality and make it possible in a short time to add something to the dishes served for the family which will make a meal worthy of a guest.

Eggs are always close at hand in most kitchens; in fact it is not unusual for a family to keep a few laying fowls in the backyard.

In Indonesia, duck eggs too are eaten. They may be used for almost every egg dish, except cakes, biscuits and sweets.

In Indonesia eggs are often preserved—duck more commonly than hen eggs. This is done by placing them in boiled water (that has been allowed to cool) mixed with powdered bricks and heavily seasoned with salt. Perhaps you have heard of the so-called Chinese hundred-year-old eggs. I have been told that they are at their best when about a hundred days old. Well, in Indonesia they are only left in the preserving solution for three weeks, long enough for the salt to soak through the pores of the shells. The eggs are then rinsed and hard-boiled, and the result is salted eggs. These salted eggs are a popular snack, sold by hawkers at bus stops and railway stations. One is enough to keep a person going for the last sixty kilometres on a slow train until he arrives home.

Omelette à la Indonesia I (Dadar telur I)

6 eggs
Salt and pepper, to taste
1 shallot, sliced into very
  thin rings

2 or 3 tablespoons oil or
  margarine

Beat eggs lightly, then season with salt and pepper. Add sliced shallots including green tops. Heat oil or margarine in an omelette pan until very hot and pour eggs in. Shake and tilt pan gently to distribute eggs over. Cook quickly until set and slightly brown. Loosen edges, turn over with omelette knife, and lightly brown the other side. Serve hot, cut in wedges.

Serves 6.

Omelette à la Indonesia II (Dadar telur II)

4 tablespoons oil or margarine
1 onion, thinly sliced
1 chilli, thinly sliced diagonally or
  1 capsicum, sliced in strips

1 tomato, thinly sliced
Salt
6 eggs

Heat 3 tablespoons oil or margarine in an omelette pan. Stir-fry onion until soft. Add chilli or capsicum, tomato slices, a pinch of salt and cook gently until tomato is soft. Beat eggs well with 1 tablespoon oil or margarine and salt. Pour eggs over. When set and brown underneath, invert carefully and turn over to cook other side. Serve hot, cut in wedges.

Serves 6.

Omelette with Prawns (Dadar telur dengan udang)

60 g (2 ounces) shelled prawns
4 tablespoons oil or margarine
4 eggs

Salt and pepper
2 tablespoons water
1 shallot, thinly sliced

Sauté shrimp in hot oil or margarine until it turns pinkish. Take out shrimp and cut into small pieces. Beat eggs lightly, season with salt and pepper, add water. Add shallots and cooked prawns to egg mixture and mix well. Make 4 omelettes or one big omelette; cut in wedges. Serve hot.

Serves 4.

Potato Omelette (Dadar telur kentang)

Oil or margarine, for frying
3 medium potatoes, peeled and
   cut into thin slices
5 eggs

Salt and pepper, to taste
2 shallot stalks, cut into
   ringlets

Heat oil or margarine in an omelette pan. Fry sliced potatoes on moderate heat, covered. Turn over a few times and fry until lightly brown but tender. Beat eggs well with salt and pepper to taste and 1 tablespoon oil or margarine. Add shallots to eggs. Pour eggs over potatoes; give a good stir to allow eggs to run underneath potato slices. Cook on moderate heat for about 90 seconds. Loosen edges and turn to cook other side. Be careful not to break the omelette. Cut into wedges and serve hot.

Serves 4.

This omelette is very tasty; it has more body than ordinary omelettes and makes the eggs go further. Adding oil into the beaten eggs ensures that there is sufficient fat to cook the other side of the omelette. Since it is heavy and a little difficult to turn, it is simpler to cook the topside under a griller.

Stuffed Omelette with Prawn Filling (Dadar isi udang)

FILLING
250 g (½ pound) shelled prawns
3 stalks spring onions
   or shallots
1 tablespoon oil or margarine

1 clove garlic
2.5 cm (1-inch) piece ginger, grated
Salt and pepper, to taste
1 tablespoon soya sauce

Devein and cut prawns in 1.5 cm (½-inch) pieces. Slice shallots or spring onions thinly. Heat margarine or oil in frying-pan and fry crushed garlic and grated ginger until fragrant. Add shrimp pieces, season with salt and pepper. Keep turning the mixture. When the prawns turn pinkish, add sliced shallots, sprinkle with soya sauce and stir-fry for 2 minutes. Remove from pan and drain, and place conveniently near the stove.

OMELETTE

6 eggs	½ cup water
½ teaspoon salt	3 tablespoons oil or margarine

Beat eggs lightly. Season with salt and pepper and stir in the water. Lightly grease a small skillet (or wok) with a drop of oil or margarine and heat. Then pour in 1 tablespoon of egg mixture. Quickly tilt pan so that the egg forms a thin layer at the bottom. It is ready when the bottom of the egg is set, but the upper surface still moist. Reduce heat to medium. Place 1 teaspoon of filling over egg. Fold egg in half to make a semi-circular shape, then press lightly along the edges to seal in filling. Turn over, lightly brown the other side. Repeat process until the egg and filling mixture are used up. Keep hot by placing on a plate set on top of a saucepan of boiling water. Arrange attractively on a platter. Decorate with parsley if you wish.

Serves 6.

Chinese Vegetable Omelettes (Pu Yung Hai)

60 g (2 ounces) or more mushrooms	6-8 shallots
3 tablespoons margarine or oil	1 cup bean sprouts (optional)
Salt and pepper	2 cabbage leaves (optional)
1 onion	5 eggs, separated
2 cloves garlic	500 g (1 pound) quick-frozen peas
250 g (8-ounce) can crab meat	1 small can tomato soup
	Water

Choose, if possible, small button-type mushrooms. Wash, drain, and slice them. Sauté in margarine until tender, adding salt and pepper to taste. Set aside. In a little margarine stir-fry chopped onion and chopped garlic until they change colour. Add crab, shallots (which have been thinly sliced, including green tops), bean sprouts, and very finely sliced cabbage leaves. Season with salt and pepper to taste. Cook vegetables evenly for 2 minutes. Remove from heat, stir in mushrooms. Stir in well-beaten egg-yolks, fold in well-beaten egg-whites. Make omelettes in usual way. This quantity will make 2 large or 4 smaller omelettes. Place them on hot platter. Scoop the hot, cooked peas around, pour over tomato sauce, made by heating tomato soup with half the soup-can of water. Serve hot with rice.

Serves 4.

Fried Eggs and Chinese Cabbage (Mata sapi dengan sawi)

6 eggs
Enough oil or margarine to
  fry eggs
1 tablespoon oil
1 onion, thinly sliced
1 head Chinese cabbage,
  cleaned and shredded
1 capsicum, cut into thin strips,
  discard seeds or 1 chilli
  diagonally sliced, discard seeds

6 stalks shallots, cut into
  5 cm (2-inch) pieces
Salt and pepper, to taste
1 cup stock
5 g (⅛ ounce) shiny type vermicelli
  (soun), just to add colour to the
  dish, soaked in hot water for
  10 minutes

Fry eggs one at a time in hot margarine. Drain on absorbent paper. Put aside, keep hot. Melt oil in frypan, stir-fry thinly sliced onion. When it changes colour, add shredded Chinese cabbage, capsicum strips and shallot pieces including green tops. Season with salt and pepper. Keep turning vegetables so that they cook evenly. Add stock when vegetables begin to shrink. Add soaked and drained vermicelli; bring to boil. Taste cabbage; if cooked remove from heat at once. Serve hot on a serving platter, with eggs arranged decoratively on top.

Serves 6.

Eggs in Fried Chilli Sauce (Telur berlada)

1 medium onion
½ cup oil
1 tablespoon ground chilli
3 tomatoes

1 chicken stock cube
Salt, to taste
6 hard-boiled eggs

Fry thinly sliced onion in hot oil. When onion changes colour, reduce heat to low. Add ground chilli, peeled, chopped tomatoes, crumbled chicken cube, salt to taste; simmer 5 minutes, stirring continuously. Add shelled eggs, simmer another 5 minutes. Turn eggs and chilli occasionally. Remove pan from heat. Cut the eggs neatly in halves with sharp knife, arrange on platter, pour over the chilli sauce. This dish goes very well with Sautéed Bean Sprouts.

Serves 4.

Marbled Eggs (Telur pindang)

10 eggs
3 tablespoons loose tea
  or 6 tea bags
2 stalks parsley
2 stalks shallots

5 cm (2-inch) piece fresh green
  ginger, thinly sliced
½ tablespoon salt
2 chicken cubes
2 tablespoons soya sauce

Make enough strong black tea to cover 10 eggs and let it stand for 10 minutes. Pour through a strainer into a saucepan with all other ingredients in it except the eggs. The saucepan should be large enough to hold all contents. Bring to the boil. Lower the heat, gently add the eggs one by one and simmer for 30 minutes. Take the eggs out and rinse, crack the shells all over gently, taking care not to break them, and strain the liquid. Return the eggs to the pan with strained liquid and continue simmering for another 20 minutes. Leave eggs to soak in the liquid for as long as possible, at least 3 hours and up to 24 hours. When peeled, the eggs will show a marbled effect where the dark brown coloured liquid has penetrated the cracked shell; at the same time it gives the eggs a wonderfully delicate flavour. These eggs can be served hot or cold. Will keep in refrigerator for several days. In Indonesia they are served as one of the components of a main meal, but they are also popular on picnics where they are convenient to carry. From an Australia point of view, they go well with a cold lunch and might even make a change as Easter eggs.

The spices used for this dish are not available in this country, but I have used my imagination in providing substitutes. The original method of preparation is maintained, however.

Eggs in Soya Sauce (Pindang telur)

6 hard-boiled eggs
4 tablespoons oil or margarine
1 large onion, thinly sliced
1 clove garlic, crushed
5 cm (2-inch) piece fresh ginger,
  sliced
1 or 2 red chillies, diagonally
  sliced, discard seeds

1 tomato, chopped
1 tablespoon sugar
½ cup water
1 tablespoon vinegar
4 tablespoons soya sauce
Salt, to taste

Shell and cut eggs in halves lengthwise, and place in a serving dish. Stir-fry in hot oil onion, garlic and ginger until onion becomes soft. Stir in chillies, tomato and sugar. Let simmer for a few minutes. Add water, vinegar and soya sauce, and slowly bring to the boil again. Salt. Check seasoning; it should taste sweet and sour. Pour sauce over the eggs.

Serves 6.

Poached Eggs in Stock *(Tumis telur)*

1 small onion, thinly sliced
1 tablespoon butter
2 cups chicken or beef stock

Salt and pepper, to taste
4 eggs
2 stalks shallots, finely chopped

In a Chinese wok stir-fry onion in hot butter until soft. Add stock and bring to boil. Season with salt and pepper to taste. Break one of the eggs and holding it as closely over the stock as possible, let it fall in. Immediately bring stock to simmering point and gently push the white over the yolk with a wooden spoon and cook for 3 to 4 minutes. Take out the egg and place in a serving dish. Maintain the water at barely simmering point and proceed with the other eggs in the same manner. The eggs should be neat and round in shape and the white should completely mask the yolk. When all the eggs are done, add the finely chopped shallots to the stock and bring mixture to the boil. Immediately pour the mixture over the eggs and serve hot.

Serves 4.

Eggs in the Nest *(Telur dalam sarang)*

3 tablespoons oil
250 g (½ pound) chicken breast, very finely shredded, 1 cm (¼-inch) strips
1 onion, grated
1 clove garlic, grated
2.5 cm (1-inch) fresh ginger, grated
Salt, to taste
30 g (1 ounce) dried or fresh mushrooms, soaked, if dried; finely shredded
1 red capsicum, quartered, sliced into thin strips; discard seeds

1 or 2 stalks shallots, very thinly sliced
1 pinch monosodium glutamate (optional)
1 teaspoon cornflour mixed with 1 tablespoon water
185 g (6 ounces) thin egg noodles (boiled and put aside)
30 g (1 ounce) butter
6 eggs
1 chicken stock cube, dissolved in ¾ cup boiling water

Heat oil and sauté chicken until it turns white. Put aside. Heat the remaining oil and stir-fry grated onion, garlic and ginger with salt until fragrant. Add mushrooms, capsicum and cook for 2 minutes. Add sautéed chicken, sliced spring onions, monosodium glutamate and cornflour mixed with water. Mix well. Check seasoning. Add boiled noodles and toss constantly to mix with chicken and vegetables. Put aside until time to use. Divide noodle mixture into six portions. Place frying pan on a low heat and brush on a little melted butter. Place one portion into pan and shape into a circle, leaving a hole in the centre, large enough for a poached egg. Break 1 egg neatly into the hole and pour 1 tablespoon hot chicken stock over the egg. Cook on medium heat until egg is done. The noodles will be crisp underneath. Keep hot in the oven. Repeat the process with the other 5 portions.

Serves 6.

This makes a perfect weekend brunch in cold weather. The noodle mixture can be prepared in advance.

Mincemeat-coated Eggs (Telur bungkus)

500 g (1 pound) topside mincemeat   1 tablespoon tamarind juice
1 onion, minced $\frac{1}{2}$ teaspoon ground coriander
2 cloves garlic, minced   1 egg, separated
Salt and pepper, to taste   4 eggs, hard-boiled, shelled
$\frac{1}{4}$ teaspoon nutmeg   Oil for deep-frying
$\frac{1}{4}$ teaspoon laos

In bowl combine minced meat with spices and egg yolk. Divide meat mixture into 4. Coat the eggs neatly with the meat mixture and dip meat balls into lightly beaten egg-white. Fry in hot oil until golden brown. Put aside. Serve in sauce (see below).

SAUCE
1 onion   1 tablespoon soya sauce
2 cloves garlic $\frac{1}{4}$ teaspoon nutmeg
1 cup beef stock (or 2 beef stock   1 tablespoon fried onion flakes
    cubes dissolved in 1 cup
    hot water)

Stir-fry onion, garlic until they are soft, but not brown. Add stock, soya sauce, nutmeg and bring to boil. Adjust seasonings. Add salt and pepper if you think it is necessary. Place balls in the sauce only to heat through. To serve, slice balls crosswise. Arrange decoratively on platter with the sauce and sprinkle fried onion flakes over.

Serves 4.

Eggs in Coconut Sauce *(Sambal goreng telur)*

1 tablespoon oil or margarine
1 onion, thinly sliced
2 cloves garlic, thinly sliced
2 chillies, cut diagonally into
  thin slices, discard seeds
1 5 cm (2-inch) piece ginger,
  thinly sliced
2 salam leaves (if available)

1 tomato, peeled and cut
  into cubes
Salt, to taste
2 cups coconut milk
$\frac{1}{4}$ teaspoon monosodium glutamate
  (optional)
6 hard-boiled eggs (shelled)

Heat oil or margarine in a large frying pan and stir-fry onion, garlic until they change colour. Add chillies, ginger, salam leaves, tomato cubes with salt to taste and cook to blend for about 1 minute. Add coconut milk, bring to boil while stirring continuously with down-up-over motion until it thickens. Add monosodium glutamate. Adjust seasoning. Add shelled eggs into the sauce and cook until eggs heat through. To serve, halve eggs, place on a serving dish and pour thick sauce on top.

Serves 6.

Dishes prepared in this way are a good start for foreigners who wish to get acquainted with Indonesian food. Prawns, some vegetables and chicken livers can all be cooked in this way. They are not hot, but have the characteristic coconut milk flavour.

Curried Eggs and Prawns *(Kari telur dengan udang)*

3 tablespoons oil
2 onions, finely sliced
2 cloves garlic, crushed
5 cm (2-inch) green ginger, finely
  sliced
500 g (1 pound) raw prawns,
  shelled and deveined
1 tablespoon curry powder
Salt and pepper, to taste
2 cups coconut milk (reconstituted
  with the blender from 125 g
  ($\frac{1}{4}$ pound) desiccated coconut in
  $2\frac{1}{2}$ cups of warm water; see
  page 17)

1 stalk lemon grass, bruised,
  or lemon rind
4 eggs, hard-boiled
4 stalks spring onions or shallots,
  cut into 5 cm (2-inch) pieces,
  including the green

Heat oil in frying pan and fry onion, garlic, and ginger until fragrant. Add prawns and sauté until pink. Take out the prawns, leave the rest. Reduce heat. Add curry powder to the pan, salt and pepper and fry gently for 2 minutes before adding the coconut milk. Bring coconut milk to boil, stirring constantly with down-up-over motion and then simmer until it thickens, for about 10 minutes. Add eggs, cut up shallots and sautéed prawns and cook for another 3-5 minutes. Do not overcook shallots. Check seasoning. Serve hot on a platter, prawns in the middle, halves of eggs as a border, and pour sauce on top.

Serves 4.

Gold and Silver Omelette in Coconut Milk (Gulai kuning dan putih telur berlapis)

2 cups coconut milk (p. 17)
1 fresh chilli, thinly sliced
   diagonally, discard seeds
1 clove garlic, crushed
1 onion, sliced
2 slices green ginger
A pinch turmeric
Salam leaf (if available)

2 chicken stock cubes, crumbled
Salt, to taste
6 eggs
1 cup water
2 tablespoons oil or margarine
8 g (¼ ounce) shiny Chinese
   vermicelli (soun)

To prepare the sauce, pour coconut milk into a saucepan. Add chilli, garlic, sliced onion, ginger, turmeric, salam leaf, crumbled chicken stock cubes and salt to taste; bring to boil while stirring constantly, otherwise coconut milk will curdle. Cook on medium heat until it thickens. Check seasonings. Let simmer. Meanwhile prepare the omelette: beat egg yolks and whites separately, each in half cup of water with salt to taste. Pour beaten egg whites into hot, well-greased omelette pan and cook on medium heat until lightly set; carefully and evenly pour in the yolk so that it forms a separate layer. When the lower layer is lightly brown, turn over omelette and lightly brown the top layer. Pour coconut milk over omelette, add vermicelli and cook on low heat for a further 2 minutes to allow the flavour of the coconut milk to be absorbed by the omelette, and the vermicelli to be heated through. Place omelette on a round serving dish with the yolk layer on top; cut into wedges. Use vermicelli as garnish and pour sauce on top. Serve hot.

Serves 6.

5 *Fish*

FISH is one of the main Indonesian sources of protein. Fresh sea fish is much used in the coastal regions and immediate hinterland, and is also popular further afield when dried and salted. On the whole, however, fresh-water fish is much more important and certainly plays a more significant role in the Indonesian diet than it does in the Australian one. There are many popular kinds: carp, perch, cat-fish and various others, and they are caught in rivers and lakes or bred in ponds or caught seasonally in wet rice fields.

An attractive feature about buying them is that often they are kept alive until the last possible moment, and the purchaser chooses his live fish from a bark tub in the market. Sometimes they are kept on crushed ice, but one thing is sure—they are that day's catch. By the late afternoon, prices fall and any unsold fish are salted and dried. Salted fish is much more economical than fresh, but some varieties are very tasty. It serves as a useful side-dish which is always available in the house, and even a little goes a long way.

Bombay Duck, its name notwithstanding, is one such form of salted fish available in this country, at least in larger food stores. It is very similar to the Indonesian dried fish, and in India is a traditional accompaniment to curry. Bombay Duck is about 13-25 cm (5-8 inches) long. It is usually fried in hot oil for about 30 seconds until it turns a pale golden colour on each side. When it is cool, it is broken into pieces about 5 cm (two inches) in length. Since, as I have mentioned, a little goes a long way! Even so, the flavour is very strong and a taste for it needs to be acquired.

Fish is cooked in a variety of ways: deep-frying, grilling on charcoal, poaching in coconut milk, or steaming. A very popular method is to season the whole fish, fold it in several layers of banana leaves, and let it cook slowly in its own juices over a charcoal fire. Although fish are often cooked as cutlets, Indonesians have a preference for cooking a fish whole, particularly for a formal meal. It makes a fine centre-piece and even has an air of dignity when complete with trimmings. When the fish is to be deep-fried however, 1.5 kg (three pounds) is the maximum size, otherwise it is too big to handle in the boiling oil.

Lemon and salt are the simplest and most popular fish seasonings, since they add freshness and character to the flavour. Star fruit and basil leaves complement the flavour very effectively and there is also a wide range of vegetables with which fish may be cooked to advantage.

Fried Fish (Goreng ikan)

1 1 kg (2-pound) fish (whole
schnapper, mullet, mackerel)
Juice of half a lemon

Salt and freshly ground black
pepper, to taste
Oil, for deep-frying

Clean, scale and trim fish. Make 2 or 3 diagonal incisions on both sides of fish with a sharp knife. Season well with salt, pepper and lemon juice. Rub the seasonings into the incisions too. Deep-fry fish until golden. For frying use enough oil to cover fish completely. Serve hot.

Serves 4.

Fried Fish in Tomato Sauce (Goreng ikan dengan kuah tomat)

1 1.5 kg (3-pound) bream (whole
with head on)
Juice of 1 lemon

Salt and freshly ground black pepper
1 egg
Flour, for coating

Clean, scale and trim fish. Make 3 or 4 diagonal incisions on both sides of fish with a sharp knife. Season well with lemon juice, salt and pepper. Rub the seasonings into the incisions too. Brush it with lightly beaten egg. Dip in flour. Shake off any surplus flour. Fry in oil or in a mixture of oil and butter until golden. Drain on absorbent paper and put aside.

SAUCE

2 small onions, thinly sliced
2 cloves garlic, thinly sliced
5 cm (2-inch) piece green ginger,
scraped and sliced
2 tablespoons margarine or oil
500 g (1 pound) tomatoes, peeled,
mashed and strained

1 teaspoon ground chilli
1 teaspoon soya sauce
1 teaspoon sugar
1 tablespoon vinegar
1 chicken stock cube, crumbled
4 shallots or spring onions,
cut in 5 cm (2-inch) lengths

Stir-fry onion slices, garlic and ginger slices in hot margarine. Cook until slices change colour. Add tomatoes and other ingredients and bring to boil. Lower heat and cook for another 10 minutes. Add spring onions 5 minutes before the sauce is ready. Pour sauce over the fish. Garnish with chilli flower and sprigs of watercress, if you wish.

Serves 4.

Fried Fish in Black Bean Sauce (Tauco ikan)

500 g (1 pound) trout or mackerel, cut into cutlets
Oil
2 onions, thinly sliced
2 cloves garlic, thinly sliced
2-3 slices green ginger
¼ teaspoon laos
2 tablespoons black bean sauce

2 capsicums, cut into fine strips, discard seeds or for those who like it hot 8 fresh hot green chillies, thinly sliced diagonally, discard seeds
2 firm tomatoes, slightly green, cut into thin wedges
Salt, to taste
1 salam leaf (if available)

Deep-fry cutlets until lightly brown. Put aside. Heat 2 tablespoons oil in a large frying pan and stir-fry onion and garlic until lightly brown. Add ginger, laos and black bean sauce, followed by capsicum strips or chilli slices and tomatoes with salt to taste and salam leaf. Since the black bean sauce is salty, add further salt with caution. Cook until vegetables wilt. Reduce heat, add fried fish, turn over a few times to coat fish with seasonings, and allow to cook until fish heats through. Place on a serving dish. Serve hot.

Serves 4.

Fried Fish in Pickled Style (Ikan cuka)

1 kg (2 pounds) fish (bonito, mullet, whiting, etc.)
Salt, to taste
Juice of 1 lemon
Oil for frying
3 onions, cut into thin wedges
2 cloves garlic, quartered

1 5 cm (2-inch) piece ginger, thinly sliced
2 fresh red chillies, whole, slit; scrape stems
2 tablespoons vinegar
2 cups water

Clean, scale, trim and cut fish into cutlets. Season well with salt and lemon. Dry-fry cutlets until lightly brown. Drain and put aside. Heat 2 tablespoons oil in a large frying pan and light stir-fry onion, garlic, ginger and chilli. Add vinegar with salt to taste. Then add water and bring to boil. Let simmer for 2 minutes. Put in the fish. Allow the flavour to soak into the fish before serving. Since this takes some time, it is best to prepare it a few hours beforehand and then reheat. Serve hot.

Serves 4.

This dish is popular because of its fresh astringent flavour which makes it go particularly well with rich dishes. The light stir-frying and the addition of vinegar before the onions are tender, ensure that they remain firm and crunchy.

Fried Fish with Tangy Dressing (Ikan acar kuning)

1.5 kg (3-pound) schnapper
Oil, to deep-fry fish

Salt, to taste
Juice of 1 lemon

SAUCE

1 medium onion, thinly sliced
3 tablespoons oil or margarine
5 candlenuts
  (or macadamia nuts)
2 cloves garlic, crushed
½ teaspoon turmeric
4 medium onions, quartered
3 red chillies, whole;
  scrape stem

1 cup vinegar
Salt, to taste
1 teaspoon sugar
2 chicken stock cubes
1 cup water
2 salam leaves (if available)

Wash and clean fish, leaving the head and tail intact; dry then lightly score the skin across diagonally on both sides to prevent cracking during cooking. Season with salt and lemon juice. Deep-fry fish until lightly golden. Place on a platter. Put aside. For frying, use enough oil to cover fish completely. To prepare sauce, stir-fry sliced onion in hot oil until slices change colour; reduce heat. Add smoothly ground candlenuts, crushed garlic and turmeric. Cook, stirring constantly, about 1 minute. Add quartered onions and chillies, vinegar, salt, sugar and stock (made by dissolving stock cubes in water). Bring to boil, stirring. Reduce heat, cook until onions are tender. Check seasoning. Pour mixture over fish.

Prepare the dish a few hours in advance to allow time to marinate. Heat up in the oven before serving. Cover loosely with a piece of aluminium foil. To serve, place on serving platter and garnish with chilli flowers and onion flowers (p. 103-4).

Serves 5.

Grilled Fish Minahasa Style (Ikan rica-rica)

1 kg (2-pound) bream (whole)	*2 onions, chopped*
3 red chillies or 1 teaspoon sambal oelek	*2 tablespoons lemon juice*
	Salt, to taste
1 5 cm (2-inch) piece ginger	*½ cup oil*
4 cloves garlic	

Clean, scale and wash the fish. Make diagonal incisions through thickest part of the body. Grind chillies, ginger, garlic and onion to a paste. Mix paste well with lemon juice and salt to taste. Stir oil into spice mixture and leave fish to marinate in this for 30 minutes. Grill the fish over charcoal or under a griller on both sides until fish is cooked, basting from time to time with the marinade. Serve hot with rice and cucumber pickle.

Serves 4.

One of my friends from Minahasa told me that she simply baked the fish, marinade and all, in the oven, saying it was less fussy, and I am inclined to agree with her.

Grilled Fish (Ikan panggang)

1.5 kg (3-pound) schnapper (whole)	*2 tablespoons soya sauce*
Salt, to taste	*2 tablespoons water*
Juice of half a lemon	*1 tablespoon butter*
2 cloves garlic, slivered	

Clean the fish. Make diagonal incisions through thickest part of the body. Season with salt and lemon juice. Combine soya sauce, water and garlic. Marinate fish in the mixture for 30 minutes. Grill the fish over charcoal or under a griller on both sides until the fish is cooked, basting it from time to time with the marinade. Smear both sides with melted butter. Place on a platter and pour the following dressing on top.

FISH DRESSING

1 tablespoon soya sauce
1 tablespoon water
1 tablespoon lemon juice
2 tablespoons fried onion
  flakes

1 fresh chilli, cut into ringlets,
  discard seeds

Combine all ingredients and pour over the grilled fish.

Serves 4.

Barbecued Fish (Panggang ikan)

4 small whole fish (1 per person,
  e.g. John Dory, trevally
  or sole)

Salt
Juice of 1 lemon

Clean and scale the fish. Score it diagonally along each side. Rub it with salt and lemon juice inside and out. Put aside.

MARINADE

2 onions
2 cloves garlic
4 fresh red chillies or
  2 teaspoons ground chilli
¼ teaspoon turmeric
2 slices green ginger
1 cup very thick coconut milk

Salt, to taste
1 stalk lemon grass; make 3 cm
  (1½-inch) horizontal cuts in the
  lower part to form a brush.
  Bruise lightly
2 tablespoons onion flakes,
  for garnish

Place onion, garlic, chilli, turmeric, ginger in blender; blend into a fine paste. Mix paste with coconut milk, salt to taste. Marinate fish in this seasoned coconut milk for 1 hour. Place fish in a grill holder; grill over a charcoal fire or under a griller basting from time to time with the remaining marinade which in the meantime has been cooking on a low heat in a small pan. Use the lemon grass brush as a dabber, for it improves the flavour. Serve hot and garnish with fried onion flakes.

Serves 4.

Baked Fish in Silver Beet (Panggang ikan bungkus)

500 g (1 pound) fish fillets
Salt, to season fish
Juice of 1 lemon
5 candlenuts or macadamia nuts
5 cm (2-inch) piece ginger, scraped
  and sliced
2 onions, thinly sliced
3 cloves garlic

$\frac{1}{4}$ teaspoon turmeric
2 chicken stock cubes
$\frac{1}{4}$ cup water
12 fresh silver beet leaves,
  cleaned, washed, left whole
2 capsicums, cut into strips,
  discard seeds
2 tablespoons snipped chives

Clean and wash fish (if using frozen fish, thaw according to directions). Brush fish with salt and lemon. Place candlenuts, ginger, onion, garlic, turmeric and chicken stock cubes with $\frac{1}{4}$ cup water in a blender and blend on medium speed until a smooth paste. Season fish fillets with the paste. Divide into four. Plunge silver beet leaves into boiling salted water; simmer for 1 minute and drain. Place each portion of seasoned fish on silver beet leaves, garnish with capsicum strips and snipped chives, and wrap into a neat package. Then wrap in foil turning ends in to secure. Do the same with the other portions. Place on a shallow baking tray and cook in a moderate oven at 180°C (350°F) for half an hour. Remove from the foil and arrange on serving platter.

Serves 4.

Padang Sour-sharp Fish (Pangek ikan)

5 candlenuts or macadamia nuts
2 onions, sliced
2 cloves garlic
8 fresh red chillies or
  1 tablespoon ground chilli
2 slices green ginger
$\frac{1}{4}$ teaspoon turmeric
500 g (1 pound) fish cutlets
  (bonito, jewfish)

Salt, to taste
2 tablespoons lemon juice
$\frac{1}{4}$ cup water
1 stalk lemon grass, bruised
$\frac{1}{4}$ lemon, cut into thin wedges;
  or 6 tiny star fruits
$\frac{1}{2}$ teaspoon monosodium
  glutamate (optional)

Grind candlenuts or macadamia nuts, onion, garlic, chilli, ginger and turmeric into a fine paste. Season fish cutlets with salt and lemon juice. Put aside. Meanwhile place chilli paste with $\frac{1}{4}$ cup of water and lemon grass with salt to taste in a thick-bottomed saucepan. Bring chilli sauce to boil. Add lemon wedges and let simmer for 5 minutes, stirring occasionally to prevent burning. Add fish cutlets, monosodium glutamate, turn over a few times to coat fish with seasoning. Cover and continue cooking on low heat until the fish is cooked (for about 20 minutes). Shake pan gently from time to time. Do not stir or the fish will crumble. Serve hot.

Serves 4.

This dish is not at its best until the day after cooking.

Wrapped Fish, Padang Style (Pangek bungkus)

1 kg (2-pound) whole fish
  (schnapper or bream)
Salt, to taste
Juice of 1 lemon
5 candlenuts or macadamia nuts
2 onions, sliced
2 cloves garlic
8 fresh red chillies or
  1 tablespoon ground chilli

1 5 cm (2-inch) piece green ginger
¼ teaspoon turmeric
1 chicken stock cube
4 basil leaves
1 stalk lemon grass, finely shredded
2 small firm tomatoes (slightly
  green), thinly sliced
6 stalks spring onions or shallots,
  cut into 5 cm (2-inch) lengths

Clean, scale and trim fish. Score the fish diagonally on both sides. Season well with salt and lemon juice. Put aside. Grind candlenuts or macadamia nuts, onion, garlic, chilli, ginger, turmeric, chicken stock cube into a fine paste. Combine nut paste, basil leaves, shredded lemon grass with salt to taste. Coat fish well with seasoning, rub into the fish inside and out. Prepare a double silver foil or banana leaves large enough to envelope fish and seasonings. Arrange half of tomato slices and shallots or spring onions as base, place fish on top and then the remaining tomato slices and shallots. Wrap neatly, turning ends in to secure. Place on a shallow baking tray and cook in a moderate oven at 180°C (350°F) for 35 minutes. Remove from the wrapping just before serving and place on a platter.

Serves 4.

Poached Fish in Mild Sauce (Gulai masin ikan)

1 kg (2-pound) fish (bonito,
  mackerel or jewfish)
Juice of half a lemon
4 cups coconut milk
3 candlenuts or macadamia nuts
2 onions, sliced thinly
4 cloves garlic

5 cm (2-inch) piece ginger, sliced
½ teaspoon turmeric
2 fresh hot chillies
4 or 5 basil leaves (if available)
Half a lemon, cut into 6 wedges
Salt, to taste

Scale, wash and slice the fish into cutlets. Season with a mixture of salt and lemon; put aside. Take 2 red chillies, stems and all. Scrape stem gently. Slice the chilli from just below the stem down to the point. Put aside. Grind macadamia nuts, ginger and garlic to a smooth paste. Place coconut milk, nut paste, chilli, turmeric, onion slices, basil leaves and salt to taste in a large saucepan to avoid overcrowding. Bring to boil stirring constantly. Leave to cook on moderate heat until the coconut milk thickens and its volume reduces by about a third. Add fish and lemon wedges and continue cooking, stirring occasionally until the fish is tender. Adjust the seasoning. To serve, arrange fish on serving dish. Pour sauce on top. Lemon wedges are not eaten.

Serves 6.

Poached Fish in Coconut Milk (Gulai ikan)

1 kg (2 pounds) fish cutlets	1 5 cm (2-inch) piece green ginger
Salt, to taste	4 cups coconut milk
Juice of 1 lemon	$\frac{1}{4}$ teaspoon turmeric
8 fresh chillies or	$\frac{1}{4}$ teaspoon laos (optional)
1 tablespoon ground chilli	1 stalk lemon grass, bruised
1 onion	2 small firm tomatoes, slightly
2 cloves garlic	green, cut into thin wedges

Season fish cutlets with salt and lemon juice. Put aside. Grind chilli, onion, garlic and ginger into a very fine paste. Place coconut milk with chilli paste, turmeric, laos, lemon grass, salt to taste in a saucepan. Bring to boil, stirring constantly with down-up-over motion to prevent coconut milk from curdling. As soon as it comes to boil, reduce the heat and let simmer for about 30 minutes until coconut milk thickens. Add fish and tomatoes; return to boil again; continue spooning coconut milk gently. Finish the cooking on medium heat until the fish is cooked and the tomatoes are tender, for about a further 10 minutes. Check seasoning. Serve hot.

Serves 6.

Herrings with Onion and Chilli Relish (Anyang sardincis)

400 g (14-ounce) tin herrings in	Juice of 1 lemon
tomato sauce	Salt, to taste
2 onions, very thinly sliced	
2 fresh red chillies, cut into very	
thin ringlets, discard seeds	

Eggs in Fried Chilli Sauce (*Telur berlada*); Prawn crackers (*Krupuk*); White Radish Relish (*Acar lobak*); Roasted Coconut with Peanuts (*Serundeng*); Chicken in Mild Sauce (*Opor ayam*)

Open tin and arrange fish on serving dish; reserve sauce. Mix together sliced onion, chilli ringlets, lemon juice, tomato sauce and salt to taste to form a relish. Spread over fish pieces; let stand for 1 hour.

Serves 4-6.

This is often served for unexpected guests in addition to what has already been prepared for a family meal. The fish is given a face-lift with the addition of a few ingredients usually handy in the kitchen. Try some in a salad roll.

Wrapped Fish, Padang Style *(Pangek bungkus)*; Assorted Boiled Vegetables; Grilled Chicken with Soya *(Ayam panggang kecap)*; Meat Minang Style *(Kalio)* with Side-dishes

6 *Other Seafood*

INDONESIANS living along the coast enjoy the choice of a wide variety of seafood—crab, lobster, prawn, and squid. In some areas, such as Bali, turtle is popular. Ways of cooking are equally varied, for this seafood may be deep-fried, stir-fried with vegetables, cooked in coconut milk or curried. In some styles of cooking the Chinese influence is quite apparent.

Prawns figure highly in the Indonesian cuisine. And whichever cooking method is chosen, they are often cooked and served in their shells. This ensures that the maximum amount of flavour is retained, and since the shell acts as an insulation against the heat, there is less risk of overcooking. In preparing the prawns for cooking, whether in or out of their shells, it is important to devein them, for the vein is gritty and unpleasant.

To devein prawns in their shells: First, rinse the prawns in lightly salted water, then remove head and strip off legs. Cut open the shell along the back with a small sharp knife and with the knife-point, remove the vein, taking care not to loosen the shell. Then rinse and dry on absorbent paper.

To shell prawns: ·Remove head, then cut along the back of the shell as above, leaving the tail shell segment intact. Then strip off shell and legs (but not tail). Afterwards, devein as above. The point in leaving the tail shell section is twofold. When the prawns are dipped in batter and deep-fried, it forms a convenient handle (also for the diner); also, visually, the brilliant red of the tail shell provides a splendid colour contrast.

King prawns are too large to fry evenly just as they are. To ensure quick, even cooking and to create a good appearance, it is useful to make them into butterfly shapes. Proceed as follows:

Shell and devein king prawns as above, leaving tail shell segment intact, then, with a sharp knife slit each prawn along its inner curve about three-quarters of its length. Spread it gently open from the inner curve outwards so that the two curves form butterfly wings. Tap lightly with the back of a spoon to make it stay flat.

To remove tail segment: Hold prawn in one hand and take its tail with finger and thumb of the other. Then squeeze firmly, pulling gently at the same time. The shell will come off easily, leaving the delicate fin-like flesh intact.

Note: For stir-frying with vegetables, small prawns are preferable, and these are best completely shelled. It must be remembered that no matter how the prawns are treated, the cooking time must be kept as brief as possible, for prolonged exposure to heat—and this is true of seafood generally—toughens the flesh and kills the flavour.

Boiled Prawns (Udang rebus)

500 g (1 pound) medium-sized green prawns

Enough water to cover prawns
Salt, to taste

Rinse prawns in lightly salted water; remove head and strip off legs. Cut open the shell along the back with a small sharp knife, and with the knife point remove the vein, taking care not to loosen the shell. Then rinse again. Pour enough water to cover prawns into a saucepan. Add salt to taste. Bring to boil. Add prawns and cook for 8 minutes. Shell prawns, but leaving the tail shell segment intact. Place on a serving dish garnished with sprigs of parsley. Serve with sauce.

SAUCE AS A DIP

1 tablespoon soya sauce
1 tablespoon vinegar or lemon juice

1 teaspoon French mustard
1 teaspoon brown sugar

Mix all ingredients thoroughly in a bowl with a fork. Diners then dip the boiled, shelled prawns into the sauce.

Serves 4.

In Indonesia this is served as one of the components of a main meal. I sometimes serve this with drinks. Keep prawn stock in the refrigerator for later use, as it is delicious for moistening stir-fried vegetables.

Fried Prawns (Goreng udang)

500 g (1 pound) green shelled
  prawns
Salt and pepper

Juice of half a lemon
Fish batter (recipe below)
Oil for frying

Devein prawns. Season with salt, pepper and lemon juice. Dip prawns in batter and drop one by one into hot oil. Fry only a few at a time until golden. Serve hot.

FISH BATTER (Adonan kulit untuk goreng ikan)

125 g (4 ounces) flour
1 egg yolk

1 cup milk
Pinch of salt

Sift the flour into a bowl and make a well in the centre. Pour in egg yolk. Stir lightly and then add milk gradually. Add salt. Beat well to make it smooth and light. Let stand for about an hour before using.

Serves 4.

Stir-fried Prawns in Coconut Milk (Sambal goreng udang)

1-2 tablespoons margarine
1 onion, chopped
2 cloves garlic, crushed
1 kg (2 pounds) green prawns
2 teaspoons ground chilli
3-4 pieces green ginger, about
  3 cm (1-inch) thick

$\frac{1}{2}$ teaspoon monosodium
  glutamate (optional)
500 g (1 pound) green beans
1 cup coconut milk (p. 17)
1 firm tomato
1 bunch shallots

Heat margarine, stir-fry onion and garlic until they change colour. Add shelled, deveined prawns, stir constantly. When half-cooked, add ground chilli, ginger, monosodium glutamate, and beans, which have been sliced diagonally, thinly, and evenly. Cook about 3 minutes; add coconut milk. Stir continually with down-up-over motion to avoid curdling; bring to boil. Add peeled, chopped tomato, shallots cut into 5 cm (2-inch) lengths, including green tops. Stir constantly. When beans are tender, remove from heat. This dish goes very well with *Serundeng*.

Serves 8.

Coconut and Prawns Baked in Foil (Pepes udang)

1 onion
2 cloves garlic
3 fresh red chillies or
   1½ teaspoons ground chilli
Pinch of turmeric
1 cup desiccated or fresh
   grated coconut

1 cup shelled, deveined
   baby prawns
Juice of half a lemon
Salt, to taste
1 firm tomato, slightly green
2 tablespoons water, to
   moisten coconut

Grind onion, garlic, chillies and turmeric into a fine paste. Moisten coconut with water. In a bowl combine prawns, chilli paste, lemon juice, moistened desiccated coconut and salt to taste. Place half of tomato slices as base on double layers of silver foil or banana leaves; spoon coconut mixture on top and then the remaining tomato slices and wrap neatly, turning ends in to secure. Place on a shallow baking tray and cook in a moderate oven at 180°C. (350°F.) for 35 minutes or cook over charcoal, turning from time to time. Remove wrapping just before serving, and place on a serving dish. Serve hot as a side-dish.

Serves 4.

Stir-fried Prawns with Long Beans and Black Bean Sauce (Tumis udang dengan kacang pandang dan tauco)

500 g (1 pound) long green beans
   (Chinese snake beans)
2 cloves garlic, crushed
1 onion, thinly sliced
5 cm (2-inch) piece green ginger,
   scraped and sliced
2 fresh chillies, thinly sliced
   diagonally, discard seeds or
   1 capsicum, sliced into thin
   strips, discard seeds

2 tablespoons oil
1 tablespoon black bean sauce
Salt, to taste
125 g (¼ pound) shrimp, shelled
   and deveined, diced if large
½ cup chicken stock or water

Wash and trim beans, break into sections about 4 cm (1½ inches) long and put aside. Stir-fry garlic, onion, ginger and chilli slices (or capsicum strips) in hot oil until fragrant. Add black bean sauce, stirring all the time. Add prepared beans and salt to taste. Stir-fry for 3 minutes, then add shrimps and stir-fry for another 2 minutes. Add stock and bring to boil. Serve hot.

Serves 4.

Sweet Corn Patties with Prawns (Pergedel jagung dengan udang)

1 470 g (15-ounce) tin whole
  kernel sweet corn
500 g (1 pound) green prawns,
  shelled, cut into small chunks
5 stalks shallots, leaves and all,
  evenly sliced

2 eggs
2 tablespoons plain flour
Salt and freshly ground pepper,
  to taste

Make corn into a pulp by putting through a mincer. Combine all ingredients thoroughly. Spoon into hot oil to deep-fry. Drain and serve hot. Sufficient for 25 or more patties. If made smaller, they are ideal for cocktail parties or receptions. They can be heated in an oven.

Serves 6.

Bean Curd Balls with Prawns (Frikadel tahu dengan udang)

4 bean curds, chopped
500 g (1 pound) green prawns,
  shelled, deveined and chopped
1 onion, chopped
2 cloves garlic, chopped
2 stalks shallots, thinly sliced

2 tablespoons chopped celery
  leaves
2 tablespoons cornflour
2 eggs, beaten
Salt and pepper, to taste
Oil, for deep-frying

Mix bean curds and prawns with all other ingredients except oil. Drop bean curd mixture into hot oil, a tablespoon at a time. Fry until golden brown. Drain on absorbent paper. Serve as savouries. In Indonesia, bean curd balls are served as a side-dish to add variety to the menu. Bean curd has a mild 'nutty' flavour, slightly bitter, like walnuts, which lingers on the tongue, and the mildness makes it an excellent base for stronger flavours of many kinds from innumerable combinations. In China and Japan bean curd is also popular, but Europeans sometimes take a while to acquire a taste for it.

Stuffed Squid (Ikan cumi-cumi pakai isi)

6 medium-sized squid,
  about 8 cm (3-inches) long

FILLING

10 large prawns, shelled,
  deveined and chopped
2 shallots, chopped, discard
  green tops

1 egg, lightly beaten
Salt and pepper, to taste

SAUCE

4 macadamia nuts or 4 candlenuts
1 onion
4 fresh red chillies or 1 heaped
  teaspoon ground chilli
2 cloves garlic
$\frac{1}{4}$ teaspoon shrimp paste,
  lightly grilled

$\frac{1}{4}$ teaspoon turmeric
$\frac{1}{4}$ teaspoon laos
2 slices green ginger
2 cups coconut milk
1 stalk lemon grass, bruised
Salt, to taste
1 tablespoon lemon juice

Remove head of squid from body and gently detach the ink sac. Take out all inner organs without cutting hood-shaped body open and wash thoroughly. Clean and rub outer skin with salt-coated cloth. Rinse and drain. Combine prawns, chopped shallots and beaten egg for filling. Season with salt and pepper to taste. Stuff squid three-quarters full with prawn mixture and secure with toothpicks. Put aside. Place nuts, onion, chillies, garlic, shrimp paste, turmeric, laos, ginger in a blender and blend on medium speed for about 30 seconds or until they become a smooth paste. Bring coconut milk with nut paste, lemon grass and salt to boil in a saucepan, stirring constantly. Add stuffed squids and return to boil. Continue cooking on low heat for about an hour or until squid is tender. Add lemon juice and serve.

Serves 6.

7 Meat Dishes

THE MAIN kinds of meat available and consumed daily in Indonesia are beef, buffalo and goat. Since Indonesia is a Muslim country, pork does not figure highly in Indonesian cuisine although of course it is eaten in non-Muslim areas such as Bali, Menado, the Maluccas and Tapanuli by non-Muslims, wherever they happen to be.

Some of these pork dishes are interesting and exciting, for example the Balinese suckling pig roasted whole, pork and vegetable combinations, pork and shell-fish combinations, pork saté (seasoned, grilled skewered pork). Since pork is outside my experience, I have regretfully decided not to include any recipes using it, even though I have heard of a vegetarian preparing excellent meat dishes judging entirely by sight and smell.

Goat meat on the other hand, though popular in Indonesia, is not generally available in this country so that in recipes where it occurs, I have regularly substituted mutton or lamb.

A meat dish does not dominate a meal in Indonesia as it does in Western countries. Although perhaps a few Indonesians may eat in the European (in particular Dutch) style, an eight-ounce steak or a couple of succulent chops set before an Indonesian for the first time are more likely to take away than to stimulate his appetite. This attitude does not derive from a desire for economy. Rather, variety of flavours and textures on a rice base is the keynote of an Indonesian meal. And so, in some meat dishes the flesh is usually cut into pieces about 5 cm (2-inches) square, and only one or two pieces, and a little sauce, are taken by each person as part of the meal. This explains why some meat recipes may appear small, even though here and there I have adapted them to Western styles of eating.

An Indonesian meal for a middle-class family, consists of at least four or five dishes to go with the rice base: these might be one or two meat or fish dishes, a vegetable dish, side-dishes such as *krupuk*, or roasted coconut with peanuts and a selection of sambals (variously flavoured chilli pastes). Protein accordingly comes from a variety of sources such as bean curd and various beans.

The general style of cooking is naturally influenced by local conditions. Refrigerators are comparatively rare in Indonesia. A housewife does or has her shopping done every day. She does not buy more meat than can conveniently be prepared for the same day. Some treatments, of course, preserve meat—this is one of the practical uses of the spices—and for some dishes, meat is dried in the sun. In addition, there are ways and means of transforming leftovers into different and appetising new guises, just as the meat remaining from a leg of lamb can be minced and put into a shepherd's pie.

Among the many ways in which an Indonesian woman shows her quality and wins a good name is by her skill in cooking, planning and the use to which she can put her raw materials, as well as the economy with which she gets her requirements from the market.

Sun-dried Meat (Dendeng)

500 g (1 pound) lean meat (topside), in 1 piece

Salt, to taste
Juice of 1 lemon

Cut meat into slices about 3 mm ($\frac{1}{8}$ inch) thick. Season with salt and lemon. Spread on a bamboo tray and put in the sun to dry. When one side is well dried, turn over and dry the other side. It takes 2 or 3 hot sunny days to dry meat into *dendeng*. When dried, keep in an airtight container and from time to time remove from container and dry in the sun again. When drying, it is wise to cover the meat with a piece of thin muslin, tucked in round the tray and held down by weights, to protect it from dust and flies, not to mention hungry kookaburras or magpies! This is usually prepared in large quantities, about 2 kg (four pounds or more) at a time, so that there is always some on hand—part of the Indonesian housewife's planning for the contingency of unexpected guests. *Dendeng* is fried or grilled.

Chillied Dendeng I (Dendeng balado)

500 g (1 pound) sun-dried meat
  (or dendeng) (p. 75)
1½ cups oil
2 onions, thinly sliced

5 or more fresh red chillies,
  coarsely pounded
Salt, to taste
Juice of half a lemon

Cut *dendeng* into 5 cm (2-inch) squares. Fry 3 or 4 pieces at a time in hot oil on a medium heat. When one side is lightly brown, turn and cook the other side. Remove and drain. Repeat the process for the remaining *dendeng*. Strain and reheat half a cup of the leftover oil. Stir-fry onion until golden. Add chilli, salt to taste, let simmer for 5 minutes or longer (to remove sharpness of chilli) stirring occasionally. Stir in lemon juice and add the fried *dendeng* and cook together on very low heat about 2 minutes.

Serves 6.

Chillied Dendeng II (Dendeng balado basah)

500 g (1 pound) fresh topside or
  round steak in one piece
  (parboiled in ¼ cup water)
1 cup oil
1 large onion, thinly sliced

1-2 tablespoons ground chilli
2 tomatoes, peeled and chopped
2 beef stock cubes
Salt, to taste

Cut meat into slices about 3 mm (⅛ inch) thick and then cut into 5 cm (2-inch) squares and season with salt. Heat the oil and fry meat pieces until brown. Take out and set aside. Strain the fat. Reheat the same fat and fry onion in it. When the onion changes colour, reduce the heat to low. Add ground chillies, peeled and chopped tomatoes, crumbled beef stock cubes, and salt to taste. Simmer for 5 minutes. Stir chilli mixture occasionally. Remove pan from heat. This dish goes very well with boiled and sautéed vegetables.

Serves 4 or more.

Sun-dried Savoury Meat (Dendeng bumbu)

500 g (1 pound) lean meat
  (topside), in one piece
4 cloves garlic, crushed
½ teaspoon laos
1 tablespoon ground coriander
½ teaspoon cummin

2 onions, grated
2 tablespoons tamarind juice
15 g (½ ounce) palm sugar
  (optional)
Freshly ground black pepper
Salt, to taste

Cut meat into slices about 3 mm ($\frac{1}{8}$ inch) thick. Mix together spices. Season the sliced meat with the spice mixture, salt to taste and let stand in the refrigerator for one night. Then put in the sun to dry (page 75).

Fried Sun-dried Savoury Meat (Goreng dendeng bumbu)

500 g (1 pound) sun-dried savoury
   meat

2 onions, thinly sliced
1½ cups oil ·

Cut *dendeng* into 5 cm (2-inch) squares. Stir-fry onions until golden brown. Drain and place on absorbent paper. In the same oil, fry *dendeng* 5 or 6 pieces at a time. Cook on medium heat until lightly brown on both sides. Drain on absorbent paper. Repeat the process for the remaining pieces of meat. Mix fried *dendeng* with onion flakes; when cool, keep in an airtight container.

Serves 6.

Dendeng with Crisp Coconut (Dendeng ragi)

500 g (1 pound) topside or rump
   steak in one piece
250 g (8 ounces) desiccated or
   2 cups grated fresh coconut
2 beef stock cubes dissolved in
   ½ cup boiling water
2 onions, grated
3 cloves garlic, crushed
1 teaspoon ground coriander

1 teaspoon ground cummin
1½ cups oil
1-2 salam leaves (if available)
1 teaspoon brown sugar
Freshly ground black pepper
   and salt
2 tablespoons tamarind juice

Cut meat into slices about 3 mm ($\frac{1}{8}$ inch) thick and cut into 5 cm (2-inch) squares. Moisten well-desiccated coconut with beef stock (beef stock cubes dissolved in boiling water). Put aside. Stir-fry onion, garlic, coriander, caraway or cummin in hot oil until fragrant. Add meat, sugar, season with salt and pepper to taste. Turn meat occasionally; reduce heat to low and cook meat until tender. Add the desiccated coconut to the meat mixture; sprinkle with tamarind juice, mix well and fry gently on low heat until meat and coconut become crisp, stirring all the time. This takes anything up to an hour. Or place in the oven and roast on low heat at 150°C (300°F) for 20-30 minutes. Stir well occasionally. When cooked, place in a colander resting on a bowl to drain away the fat. Then place on absorbent paper to absorb any remaining excess fat before storing it in an airtight container.

Serves 8.

This dish is tasty and not hot. It will go with any vegetable dish. The method of placing the mixture in the oven to finish the cooking is the simplest.

Fried Savoury Meat (Empal daging Jawa)

500 g (1 pound) topside in one
  piece
2 teaspoons coriander
2 cloves garlic, crushed
Salt and pepper, to taste

1 tablespoon tamarind juice
$\frac{1}{4}$ cup water
$\frac{1}{2}$ cup oil
2 tablespoons fried onion flakes

Cut the meat into 3 mm ($\frac{1}{8}$-inch) thick 5 cm (2-inch) squares. Season meat pieces with the mixture of coriander, garlic, salt, pepper and tamarind juice. Cook seasoned meat with $\frac{1}{4}$ cup water until all liquid is absorbed. Then fry meat in a frying pan in hot oil until brown. Place on a serving dish and sprinkle fried onion flakes on top.

Serves 4.

This goes well with tangy vegetable dish *Sayur asam Jawa* (p. 36) served with rice.

Braised Beef Slices (Lapis daging)

500 g (1 pound) rump steak in
  one piece
2 tablespoons soya sauce
Freshly ground black pepper,
  to taste
3 cloves garlic, crushed
$\frac{1}{4}$ teaspoon nutmeg

2 onions, thinly sliced
1 tablespoon butter, margarine
  or oil
$\frac{1}{4}$ cup beef stock
2 tomatoes, puréed
Salt, to taste
1 egg, lightly beaten

Cut meat into slices about 3 mm ($\frac{1}{8}$-inch) thick and then cut into 5 cm . (2-inch) squares. Season meat slices with the mixture of soya sauce, ground pepper, garlic and nutmeg. Allow to marinate for 1 hour. Stir-fry onion in hot butter in a large frying pan until soft. Add meat slices, marinade and all, and stir-fry for 1 minute. Add stock, tomato purée and salt to taste and cook on low heat until the meat is tender. Check seasoning. Add lightly beaten egg just before finishing the cooking. Serve hot.

Serves 6.

Braised Beef in Soya Sauce (Smoor daging)

2 onions, thinly sliced
2 slices green ginger
2 cloves garlic, chopped
2 tablespoons oil or margarine
1 kg (2 pounds) round or chuck steak
2 tablespoons soya sauce
1 teaspoon brown sugar (optional)

1 cup hot water
2 tomatoes, puréed and strained
2 whole cloves
½ teaspoon nutmeg
Salt and freshly ground pepper, to taste
Fried onion flakes

Stir-fry onion, ginger and garlic in oil until soft. Add beef slices and brown on all sides. Add soya sauce (and sugar) and coat meat well. Add hot water, tomato purée, cloves, nutmeg, salt and pepper to taste, and let simmer until meat is tender. Check seasoning and serve hot. Place on a serving dish, sprinkle with fried onion flakes before serving.

Serves 8.

Braised Beef Steak (Bistik daging)

1 kg (2 pounds) rump steak or topside in one piece
2 tablespoons soya sauce
1 tablespoon tamarind juice or vinegar
¼ teaspoon nutmeg

1 teaspoon salt
Freshly ground pepper, to taste
2 tablespoons butter or margarine
½ cup boiling water or stock
2 tablespoons fried onion flakes

Pound beef lightly with the edge of a cleaver and prick all over with a fork. Combine soya sauce, tamarind juice, nutmeg, salt and pepper to taste. Rub mixture into meat. Let stand for 1 hour. Heat butter or margarine in heavy pan. Brown beef quickly on all sides. Keep marinade. Add boiling water or stock to beef and bring to boil again. Simmer, covered until beef is tender (for about 1½-2 hours). Take out beef and place on a serving dish. Add marinade to pan, return gently to boil. Check seasoning. Strain sauce and pour over beef. Sprinkle with fried onion flakes. Serve hot or cold. *Bistik* will go well with Green Bean and Bean Sprout Salad (p. 38).

Serves 4 or 6.

Beef Pot a la Padang (Pangek daging)

3 tablespoons ground red chilli
  or about 15 fresh red chillies
2 onions, quartered
3 cloves garlic
1 7 cm (3-inch) piece ginger
4 candlenuts or macadamia nuts
1½ cups water

1 stalk lemon grass, bruised
  or 1 lemon leaf
3 large tomatoes, puréed
Salt, to taste
1.5 kg (3 pounds) round steak or
  topside, in the piece

Grind chilli, onions, garlic, ginger and candlenuts into a very fine paste.
Mix the chilli paste with 1½ cups water. Add lemon grass, tomato purée
and salt to taste. Pour over beef placed in a thick-bottomed saucepan.
Bring to boil. Shake saucepan from time to time to prevent it burning.
Put the lid on and continue cooking on a low heat, stirring from time
to time until the meat is tender, for about 3 hours. Serve hot with
stir-fried vegetables and boiled rice.

Serves 6-8.

This may appear from the ingredients to be hot, but the slow cooking
removes any sharpness and blends the flavours that are sharp, positive and
well defined.

Meat Balinese Style (Daging masak Bali)

500 g (1 pound) topside or rump
  steak in the piece
1 tablespoon ground chilli or
  6 fresh red chillies
½ teaspoon shrimp paste
1 brown onion, quartered
3 cloves garlic

1 5 cm (2-inch) piece green ginger
Salt, to taste
2 tablespoons oil
2 tablespoons soya sauce
1 teaspoon brown sugar
1 tablespoon lemon juice

Cut meat into slices about 3 mm (⅛ inch) thick, then cut into 5 cm (2-inch)
squares. Put aside. Place chillies, shrimp paste, quartered onion, garlic,
ginger and salt in a blender with oil. Blend on medium speed until
mixture is smooth, about 30 seconds. Stir-fry the paste in a frying pan
on medium heat until fragrant for about 2 minutes. Add the meat slices
and stir-fry until they change colour. Add soya sauce, brown sugar and
lemon juice. Continue cooking on low heat while stirring occasionally
until meat is tender. Check seasonings. Serve hot.

Serves 4.

Meat Minang Style (Kalio)

This is a dish which requires care and attention during cooking so that the mixture does not curdle. It is not worth the trouble to make it in small quantities; whatever remains can be reheated again and again, thereby gaining in concentrated flavour each time.

When making *Kalio* for the first time, you may like to use a little less than the 250 g (8 ounces) of ground chillies mentioned below—30-90 g (2 or 3 ounces) might be better. However, those who enjoy the rich, spicy flavour of Indonesian food, will use the full amount.

2 onions, quartered
8 cloves garlic
4 tablespoons ground chillies
½ teaspoon turmeric
½ teaspoon laos
7 cm (3-inch) green ginger
Salt, to taste
3 kg (6 pounds) topside steak

2 stalks lemon grass
(2 teaspoons dried lemon grass)
2 lemon leaves (whole)
1 turmeric leaf (whole)
1½ kg (3 pounds) desiccated coconut
(to make about 20 cups or 5 litres
thick coconut milk)

Place quartered onions, garlic, ground chillies, turmeric, laos, skinned sliced ginger and salt into blender; add 4 tablespoons of water. Blend on medium speed until mixture is smooth, about 30 seconds. It may be necessary to blend again to ensure smoothness. Cut meat into 5 cm (2½-inch) cubes. Season meat pieces with half the blender mixture. Put aside. Make coconut milk from desiccated coconut (p. 17). Add remaining spice mixture, lemon grass, lemon leaves and turmeric leaf to coconut milk in saucepan. Bring to boil, stirring it with down-up-over motion. It is important that this be stirred or spooned continuously or it will curdle. Once the coconut milk reaches boiling point, reduce heat to medium; continue cooking until mixture thickens, i.e. when a film of mixture remains on a spoon dipped into it. This may take 1 hour. Now add meat with spices; bring to boil again, stirring and spooning continually. Once mixture comes to boil, reduce heat, cook gently until meat is tender (approximately 1 hour). Serve hot in a serving dish.

Serves 12-16.

Rendang (Rendang)

Everything as above until *Kalio* stage is complete. *Kalio* marks the first step in the preparation of *Rendang*, which is in fact, *Kalio* cooked on a very low heat until the broth has almost dried out and a dark brown residue surrounds the crisp meat. In *Kalio*, the meat and the sauce complement each other, but in *Rendang* the residue is also an equally important part of the dish.

Quite often, the mother of a large family will help the meat go further by adding kidney beans or small potatoes in their jackets (about 2 cm (¾-inch) in diameter), lightly slit, to let in the flavour. If she plans to do so, she takes it into account when deciding how much coconut milk she needs.

It is difficult to describe what makes *Rendang* rendang. What I think happens is something like this. As the cooking proceeds and the coconut milk becomes oil, it is absorbed into the pieces of meat; and with the constant gentle heat, the meat actually fries from inside. This is what gives a suggestion of crispness to the richness of the flavour, and makes the inside of the meat so smoothly and evenly cooked.

What is Curry?

Curry is a word frequently used by foreigners to describe Indonesian dishes cooked with coconut milk. I am not sure how broad a meaning 'curry' has, but to me it is something quite specific—a preparation made of cardomom seed, cummin seed, cinnamon bark, cloves and so on, with a distinctive aroma and flavour. And curry is a word with a definite connotation usually used in reference to dishes of Arab or Indian origin.

There are many original Indonesian dishes cooked with coconut milk and spices of various kinds which include none of these ingredients, therefore in such cases I have avoided using the word 'curry' to describe them.

Lamb Curry I (Kurmah)

INGREDIENTS TO BE GROUND INTO PASTE

2 tablespoons coriander
1 teaspoon cummin seed
1 kg (2 pounds) boned leg of lamb
3 tablespoons oil or ghee
3 onions, thinly sliced
6 cloves garlic, finely chopped
1 piece cinnamon, 5 cm (2 inches) long
4 cloves

10 white peppercorns
6 candlenuts or macadamia nuts
2 cardomom pods, broken open
1 stalk lemon grass
1 5 cm (2-inch) piece ginger, thinly sliced
Salt, to taste
4 cups coconut milk
Juice of 1 lemon

Cucumber Salad *(Slada mentimun)*; Braised Beef in Soya Sauce *(Smoor daging)*; Meat and Potato Croquettes *(Pergedel kentang dengan daging)*

Grind the spices to be ground in an electric blender or a mortar into a smooth paste. Cut meat into bite-sized pieces. Heat oil in a large pan

and fry sliced onions and garlic until slightly brown; then add cinnamon, cloves, cardomom, lemon grass, ginger and the finely ground ingredients. Add meat pieces with salt to taste, coating well with the cooked spices. Leave to cook on moderate heat for 5 minutes, turning meat over a few times. Pour in coconut milk and bring to boil, stirring constantly with down-up-over motion. Reduce heat and let simmer while stirring occasionally until meat is tender and the broth thickens. Add lemon juice just before finishing the cooking. Adjust the seasoning and serve hot.

Serves 8.

This dish is served with plain boiled rice, but is also good eaten with *Roti djala* (lace pancake; *djala* means casting net). *Roti djala* when cooked looks like a pancake with holes, just like a net. (See recipe below.)

Lace Pancake (curry accompaniment) (Roti djala)

315 g (10 ounces) sifted flour
1 pinch of salt
2 eggs

4 cups coconut milk
2 tablespoons oil or butter

Put flour and salt in a bowl. Add eggs. Stir in the flour gradually from the sides. Add the coconut milk a little at a time. When half the coconut milk is used and the flour moistened, beat well to remove all lumps and to make it light. When quite smooth, add the remainder of the coconut milk gradually. Lightly brush heated omelette pan with oil or butter. Hold a perforated ladle over the pan with one hand and pour one small ladle of batter into it with the other. Quickly rotate the perforated ladle round the pan. Cook till nicely set, but not brown. Remove and keep warm on a plate. Repeat the process until all the batter is used.

Lamb Curry II (Gulai kambing)

1 kg (2 pounds) boned leg of lamb
3 cloves garlic
1 5 cm (2-inch) piece ginger
1 tablespoon ground chilli
1 tablespoon ground coriander
1 teaspoon ground cummin
½ teaspoon turmeric
¼ teaspoon nutmeg·
2 tablespoons oil
2 onions, thinly sliced

3 cloves
1 piece cinnamon stick,
   5 cm (2 inches) long
1 stalk lemon grass, bruised
Salt, to taste
2 tomatoes, puréed
4 cups coconut milk
½ cup grated fresh coconut or
   desiccated coconut, made into
   coconut butter (p. 12)

Meat Minang Style *(Kalio)* with Rice

Cut meat into bite-sized pieces. Put aside. Grind garlic, ginger and chilli finely in a blender. Add ground coriander, caraway or cummin, turmeric, nutmeg, and grind together to a smooth paste. Heat oil in a large saucepan and fry onion until lightly browned. Add the smooth paste, clove, cinnamon stick and lemon grass. Fry a little, then add meat pieces and salt to taste, coating well with the cooked spices. Add tomato purée. Leave to cook on moderate heat for 5 minutes, turning meat mixture a few times. Add coconut milk and bring to boil stirring constantly with down-up-over motion. Add the coconut butter and continue cooking on medium heat until the meat is tender. Check seasoning before removing from heat. Serve hot.

Serves 8.

Tasty Mince, Javanese Style (Podomoro)

2 onions	2 tablespoons oil
3 cloves garlic	Salam leaf (if available)
2 candlenuts or macadamia nuts	1 stalk lemon grass, bruised
1 tablespoon coriander	500 g (1 pound) minced steak
$\frac{1}{4}$-$\frac{1}{2}$ teaspoon ground chilli	Salt, to taste
$\frac{1}{2}$ teaspoon laos	1 cup coconut milk

Place onion, garlic, nuts, coriander, chilli and laos in a blender with oil and blend into a smooth paste. Stir-fry paste, salam leaf and lemon grass until fragrant for about 4-5 minutes. Add minced meat and salt to taste, stirring, and cook until it changes colour. Add coconut milk, bring to boil while stirring constantly and cook on low heat until meat is tender. Serve hot.

Serves 4.

In Indonesia this is served with boiled rice in the same way as other dishes. Try some on spaghetti as a substitute for Bolognaise sauce.

Savoury Meat Loaf (Gadon)

1 kg (2 pounds) minced steak	1 tablespoon lemon juice
2 onions, minced	$\frac{1}{4}$ teaspoon laos
2 cloves garlic, minced	2 beaten eggs
1 tablespoon ground coriander	Salt and freshly ground pepper,
$\frac{1}{4}$ teaspoon ground cummin	to taste

Combine all ingredients in a bowl. Stir with a fork till well mixed. Place in a heatproof dish, press lightly until smooth on top then steam until meat is cooked through. Serve hot. In Indonesia it is steamed in single servings, wrapped neatly in banana leaves.

Serves 8.

Meat Croquettes (Pergedel daging)

500 g (1 pound) finely minced
  hamburger steak
2 slices of bread, finely crumbled
2 eggs, separated
2 shallots, finely chopped,
  green tops and all
2 cloves garlic, minced

2.5 cm (1-inch) piece ginger,
  finely grated
½ teaspoon nutmeg
1 tablespoon lemon juice
Salt and pepper, to taste
Oil for frying

In a bowl combine meat, finely crumbled bread, egg yolks, shallots, garlic, ginger, nutmeg, lemon juice, salt and pepper to taste. Form meat mixture into oval patties 1.5 cm (½ inch) thick and 5 cm (2 inches) long. Knead firmly. Beat egg whites lightly with a fork in a small bowl. Dip meat patties one at a time in egg white; the egg white will form a covering skin and prevent croquettes from breaking up. Deep-fry in hot oil until golden brown. Serve hot and garnish with parsley.

Serves 4.

These are ideal for cocktail savouries if made smaller.

Fried Liver (Goreng hati)

500 g (1 pound) calf's liver, cut
  into slices about 1.5 cm (½-inch)
  thick
Flour, to coat

Salt and pepper, to taste
Oil for frying
½ cup fried onion flakes

Remove membrane and veins from slices of liver. Dip in flour seasoned with salt and pepper. Fry in hot oil on both sides until done. Allow about 2 minutes for 1.5 cm (½-inch) thick slices, for each side to cook. Do not overcook. Serve hot, sprinkled with onion flakes.

Serves 4.

Seasoned Braised Liver (Hati masak bumbu)

500 g (1 pound) calf's liver, cut into
   slices about 1.5 cm (½ inch) thick
Salt and pepper, to taste
1 teaspoon coriander
1 onion, thinly sliced
2 cloves garlic
2 slices ginger
60 g (2 ounces) butter or margarine
½ cup beef stock or 1 stock cube
   dissolved in ½ cup hot water
1 tablespoon tamarind juice

Remove membrane and veins from slices of liver. Season liver slices with salt, pepper and coriander. Put aside. Stir-fry onion, garlic and ginger in butter until soft but not brown. Add seasoned liver and stir-fry quickly until they change colour. Add stock and tamarind juice; check seasonings. Cover and cook till tender for about 15 minutes. Serve hot.

Serves 4.

Braised Liver in Soya Sauce (Semur hati)

500 g (1 pound) calf's liver, cut into
   slices about 1.5 cm (½ inch) thick
Salt and pepper, to taste
2 tablespoons soya sauce
¼ teaspoon nutmeg
1 onion, thinly sliced
2 cloves garlic
60 g (2 ounces) butter or margarine
½ cup beef stock or 1 stock cube
   dissolved in ½ cup hot water
½ cup tomato purée
½ teaspoon brown sugar
½ cup fried onion flakes

Remove membrane and veins from slices of liver. Season liver slices with salt, pepper, soya sauce and nutmeg. Put aside. Stir-fry onion and garlic in hot butter or margarine until soft, but not brown. Add seasoned liver and stir-fry quickly until it changes colour. Add stock and tomato purée. Check seasonings, add sugar. Cover and cook till tender, for about 15 minutes. Serve hot with onion flakes sprinkled on top.

Serves 4.

Fried Beef Tripe (Goreng babat)

750 g (1½ pounds) tripe
Juice of 1 lemon
Salt, to taste
2 cups vegetable oil
2 medium onions, thinly sliced
2 chillies, diagonally thinly
   sliced, discard seeds
¼ cup (2 ounces) butter or oil

Put tripe in saucepan, cover with water and cook until tender. Drain off water. Cut tripe into 5 cm (2-inch) squares. Marinate in lemon juice and salt for 10 minutes. Take out tripe and fry it in hot oil until golden brown. Mix tripe with onions and chillies, which have been fried in butter. If you wish, the chillies can be omitted, but in this case the tripe must be seasoned with freshly ground pepper before frying. Many people don't care for tripe, but Indonesians cook it in the most delicious way. Ask your butcher for veal tripe and buy it ready soaked and boiled from the butcher. Remember, cooked tripe should always remain very slightly resistant to the teeth.

Serves 6.

Tripe with Coconut Milk (Gulai babat)

750 g (1½ pounds) tripe	1 large onion
1 tablespoon ground hot chillies	½ teaspoon monosodium glutamate
5 cm (2-inch) piece green ginger	1 stalk lemon grass (whole)
½ teaspoon turmeric	or grated lemon rind
½ teaspoon laos	2 cups of thick coconut cream
3 cloves garlic	1 leek, thinly sliced

Place tripe in saucepan, cover with water and cook on low heat for an hour. Drain off water, then cut tripe into 5 cm (2-inch) squares. If fresh ingredients are used, put chillies, green ginger, turmeric, laos, garlic, onion in a blender and make into a fine paste. Put paste, monosodium glutamate and lemon grass in a saucepan with tripe and coconut milk. Salt to taste. Bring to the boil and stir continuously. Lower the heat and simmer until the sauce thickens, while stirring frequently. Add leek slices 10 minutes before taking it off the heat. The cooking time is about 1 hour or longer, but do not cook until it becomes a repellent slithery mass. Serve hot.

Serves 6 or more persons.

Braised Ox Tongue in Soya Sauce (Smoor lidah)

1 unsalted ox tongue	2 tablespoons soya sauce
5 cups water	½ teaspoon nutmeg
1 tablespoon salt	½ teaspoon freshly ground
4 cloves	black pepper
1 small stick cinnamon	2 tomatoes, puréed and strained
2 onions, thinly sliced	½ teaspoon monosodium glutamate
3 cloves garlic, crushed	(optional)
4 tablespoons butter or margarine	Salt, to taste

Curl the tongue into a saucepan. Add water, salt, cloves and cinnamon stick. Bring to boil, cover and simmer for 2 or 3 hours until the tongue is tender. Allow to cool. Lift out of pan, then trim and skin. Sauté onions and garlic lightly in butter. Take out of pan, but leave fat. In the same fat brown tongue on all sides. Add soya sauce, nutmeg, ground pepper, strained tomatoes, onions, garlic, monosodium glutamate and salt to taste. Braise gently for 15 minutes. Check seasoning. Serve hot. Place whole tongue on a serving dish and cut several thin slices. Pour sauce on top and garnish with crisp onion flakes.

Serves 6 or more persons.

8 Poultry

CHICKEN is highly regarded in Indonesia and a chicken dish is always a mark of honour if served to a guest. Such a guest may quite likely be the mother-in-law. And if a mother-in-law says of her reception, 'Baru saja saya di pintu, ayam terkeok di belakang' ('Hardly had I stepped in the door than there was the squawk of a slaughtered fowl at the back), this means she thinks the daughter-in-law honours her and, as a wife, is worthy of her son.

It should be remembered that in Indonesia, chicken dishes involve a lot of work if chickens are kept and allowed to run loose, and little effort is saved if they are bought in the market, then slaughtered at home according to the Muslim ritual, plucked and cleaned. Labour-saving frozen chickens are virtually unknown there, but here, a frozen chicken thawed in the usual manner puts the preparation of all these dishes at one's finger-tips.

A housewife can show her skill by the uses to which she is able to put the chicken, for it can produce at least three dishes: the liver and gizzard cut up very finely to be stir-fried with vegetables; the breast and legs for deep-frying; wing, neck and so on for broth. On special occasions there are other possibilities; one of these is Spiced Spread-eagled Chicken which is served with Festive Yellow Rice on ceremonial occasions, such as wedding feasts and circumcisions.

Braised Chicken, Balinese Style (Ayam masak Bali)

1.25 kg (2½-pound) chicken
1 onion
2 cloves garlic
2 fresh red chillies or
    1 teaspoon ground chilli
4 macadamia nuts or candlenuts
1 5 cm (2-inch) piece green ginger,
    sliced

1 cup water
2 tablespoons oil
½ teaspoon brown sugar
1 tablespoon soya sauce
1 tablespoon white vinegar
Salt, to taste

Cut chicken into serving pieces or, if left whole, split chicken in half through breast and flatten it out. Place onion, garlic, chilli, nuts and ginger with 2 tablespoons of water in a blender and blend on medium speed until all seasoning becomes a smooth mixture. Heat oil in a large frying pan and stir-fry nut mixture on medium heat until fragrant, for about 30 seconds. Put in chicken pieces and turn over a few times to coat with seasonings. Add water (preferably hot), sugar, soya sauce and vinegar; stir well and continue cooking with the lid on until the chicken is tender. Stir occasionally. Salt to taste and serve hot.

Serves 5.

Braised Chicken, Minahasa Style (Ayam Masak di buluh)

1 1.5 kg (3-pound) chicken	*3 stalks shallots, finely chopped,*
Salt, to taste	*green and all*
3 onions, thinly sliced	*1 stalk lemon grass*
5 tomatoes, cut into wedges	*1 lemon leaf*
1 tablespoon ground chillies	*1 cup water*
1 tablespoon ground green chillies	*1 teaspoon monosodium glutamate*
	(optional)

Cut chicken into serving pieces, season with salt and pepper and place in a pan with all other ingredients. Bring to boil. Check seasoning. Reduce heat and cover pan; let simmer for 30 minutes or until chicken is tender. Shake pan occasionally instead of stirring.

Serves 4.

Traditionally, this dish is cooked in a bamboo container (*buluh* means bamboo) over a charcoal fire, turning several times until chicken is tender.

I have noticed that if chilli and white pepper are cooked together, the resulting taste is a particularly stinging kind of pungency. But this is in character for some dishes. See Braised Duck with Green Chilli.

Braised Chicken in Soya Sauce (Smoor Ayam)

1 plump 1.5 kg (3-pound) roasting	*Juice of 1 lemon*
chicken	*Oil, for deep-frying*
Salt and pepper, to taste	

BROTH

2 onions, thinly sliced
3 cloves garlic, chopped
2 tomatoes, puréed and strained
3 tablespoons soya sauce
60 g (2 ounces) margarine
8-10 peppercorns

2 chicken cubes
½ teaspoon nutmeg
2 cups water
Salt, to taste
15 g (½ ounce) shiny type vermicelli, soaked in hot water

Cut chicken into serving pieces. Season well with salt, pepper and lemon juice. Deep-fry in hot oil until golden. Take out chicken and put aside. BROTH: Stir-fry onion and garlic until light brown. Add water and all other ingredients except vermicelli. Bring to boil. Add chicken pieces to broth. Let simmer for 5 minutes. Correct seasoning. Add vermicelli a few minutes before the end of cooking time. Heap chicken in the middle of a serving dish and spread vermicelli around the chicken.

Serves 6.

Chicken Curry (Gulai ayam)

1 plump chicken, about 1.5 kg (3 pounds)
3 cloves garlic
1 5 cm (2-inch) piece ginger, sliced
5 fresh red chillies or 1 tablespoon sambal oelek
2 onions, thinly sliced
1 tablespoon oil
2 cloves
1 small piece cinnamon bark

1 teaspoon ground coriander
¼ teaspoon turmeric
Salt, to taste
4 cups coconut milk
1 stalk lemon grass
1 lemon leaf (if available)
Juice of half a lemon
½ cup desiccated or freshly grated coconut

Cut cleaned chicken into serving pieces. Put aside. Grind garlic, ginger and chillies into a fine paste. Stir-fry onion in hot oil until soft. Reduce heat and add cloves, cinnamon stick, chilli paste mixture, ground coriander, caraway, turmeric and cook all together for 1 minute. Add chicken pieces and salt to taste, and coat well with the cooked spices. Stir in the coconut milk, add lemon grass and lemon leaf, bring to boil while stirring continuously with down-up-over motion. Add the coconut butter made from the coconut and continue cooking on a medium heat until the chicken is tender. Add lemon juice and check seasoning before finishing the cooking. Serve hot.

COCONUT BUTTER: Brown grated or desiccated coconut in a frying pan on low heat stirring constantly. Remove from heat. While hot grind to a smooth fine paste. It is this coconut butter which gives the unique and characteristic flavour to curry dishes.

Serves 6.

Chicken 'Gule' (Gulai ayam)

1 1.5 kg (3-pound) chicken
2 onions, sliced
3 cloves garlic, chopped
5 candlenuts or 5 macadamia nuts
2 tablespoons ground hot chilli
½ teaspoon turmeric
7 cm (3-inch) piece green ginger, scraped and sliced
¼ teaspoon laos

Salt, to taste
1 piece lemon grass
1 lemon leaf (if available)
4 cups coconut milk (p. 17)
1 small fresh pineapple, diced, preferably not quite ripe
½ teaspoon monosodium glutamate (optional)

Cut cleaned chicken into serving pieces. Put aside. Grind sliced onions, garlic, candlenuts, chilli, turmeric, green ginger and laos into fine paste. Place the paste, salt, lemon grass, lemon leaf with coconut milk in a pan. Bring to boil slowly, while stirring with down-up-over motion. Add chicken pieces, stirring continuously until mixture returns to the boil. When chicken is half-done, add diced pineapple and monosodium glutamate; let simmer until chicken is tender. Check seasoning before serving.

Serves 4 or more persons.

Chicken in Mild Sauce (Opor ayam)

1 plump chicken
4 candlenuts or macadamia nuts
7 cm (3-inch) piece green ginger, finely chopped
2 onions, finely chopped
3 cloves garlic, finely chopped
2 tablespoons coriander
½ teaspoon ground laos

½ teaspoon cummin
1 piece lemon grass
2 salam leaves (if available)
2 tablespoons oil
Salt and pepper, to taste
4 cups coconut milk
2 tablespoons tamarind juice

Cut chicken into serving pieces. Grind candlenuts, green ginger, onions and garlic into a fine paste. Stir-fry the paste, coriander, laos, cummin, lemon grass, and salam leaves in hot oil in a large saucepan to bring out the flavour and aroma of the spices. Add chicken pieces, season with salt and pepper. Stir well; cover saucepan and let simmer for 10 minutes. Add coconut milk and slowly bring to boil. Stir coconut milk with down-up-over motion to stop it from curdling. Cook over medium heat until the chicken is tender. Correct seasoning; add tamarind juice just before finishing the cooking.

Serves 4.

Chicken Pot, Padang Style (Pangek ayam Padang)

1 plump 1.5 kg (3-pound) chicken	*½ teaspoon turmeric*
3 onions, thinly sliced	*1 stalk lemon grass*
3 cloves garlic	*1 lemon leaf (optional)*
3 tablespoons ground chilli	*4 tomatoes, puréed, strained*
4 candlenuts (optional)·	*Salt, to taste*
1 7 cm (3-inch) piece ginger	*1 cup water*

Cut cleaned chicken into 4 pieces. Place in large, thick-bottomed saucepan. Grind onions, garlic, chilli, candlenuts and ginger into very fine paste. Mix the paste and all the other ingredients with water and pour over chicken pieces in saucepan. Shake saucepan and bring to boil. Put the lid on and continue cooking on a low heat until meat is tender. Check seasoning before serving.

Serves 4.

Crisp Fried Chicken (Goreng ayam)

1.25 kg (2½-pound) chicken	*Juice of 1 lemon*
Salt and pepper, to taste	*Oil, for deep-frying*

Cut chicken (bones and all) into 8 pieces, each approximately the same size. Season chicken well with salt, pepper and lemon juice. Deep-fry chicken, a few pieces at a time, until golden brown. Serve hot on platter and sprinkle crisp, fried onions on top so that chicken will not look 'undressed'. This chicken is best eaten with the fingers.

Serves 2 or more persons.

Fried Chicken with Chilli (Goreng ayam balado)

1.25 kg (2½-pound) chicken	*2 onions, very thinly sliced*
Salt, to taste	*2 tablespoons coarsely ground chilli*
Juice of 1 lemon	*2 tomatoes, chopped*
Oil, for deep-frying	*1 chicken cube*

Cut cleaned chicken, bones and all, into serving pieces. Season well with salt and lemon. Deep-fry, a few pieces at a time, until golden brown. Take out and put aside. Strain and pour back into frying pan about $\frac{1}{4}$ cup of the used oil. Heat up oil again and fry onions until lightly brown. Add chilli and tomatoes. Stir, to stop from burning. Reduce heat; add broken up chicken cube and salt to taste. Let simmer for 3 minutes. Add chicken pieces and mix with chilli mixture thoroughly. Best served while hot. This goes well with plain boiled rice and boiled vegetables.

Serves 4.

Grilled Chicken with Soya (Ayam panggang kecap)

1.25 kg (2½-pound) roasting
  chicken
3 tablespoons soya sauce
Juice of 1 lemon
Black pepper, to taste

3 cloves garlic, minced
3 tablespoons safflower or your
  favourite oil, or melted butter

Split cleaned, trimmed chicken through the back and flatten bird. Lightly mix soya sauce, lemon juice, pepper, garlic and oil with a fork and season the chicken generously with this mixture. Grill over charcoal or under a griller for about 30 minutes, turning the chicken occasionally and basting frequently with leftover seasoning. Indonesians serve this hot together with other dishes and rice. I sometimes also serve it with vegetable salad and bread rolls. Only very young and tender chickens can be cooked in this way.

Serves 2 or more persons.

Roast Chicken with Saté Flavour (Ayam panggang) bumbu saté)

1 tablespoon ground chilli
1 tablespoon coriander
½ teaspoon ground cummin seed
2 candlenuts
5 cm (2-inch) piece ginger
½ teaspoon turmeric
2 onions, thinly sliced
3 cloves garlic, crushed

¼ cup oil
Salt, to taste
1.25 kg (2½ pound) roasting chicken
1 stalk lemon grass
2 cups very thick coconut milk
  (type I)
1 dessertspoon tamarind juice

Pound chillies, coriander, cummin seed, candlenuts, ginger from which you have scraped the skin and turmeric into a very fine paste. (Or place ingredients in blender with 3 tablespoons of water. Blend on medium speed until all ingredients become a smooth mixture.) Sauté onion and garlic in hot oil until transparent. Stir in the paste, salt to taste and sauté until fragrant for about 2 minutes, stirring to prevent it burning. Remove pan from heat and put aside to cool. When cool, rub chicken inside and out with seasoning. Place chicken in a roasting pan. Add the remaining seasoning to the coconut milk and bring to the boil while stirring; let simmer for 10 minutes. Add tamarind juice and pour the coconut milk mixture gently over the chicken. Roast in moderate oven at 180°C (350°F) for about 1 hour or until done, basting occasionally. Chicken should be nicely browned and the gravy thick.

Serves 4.

Savoury Fried Chicken, Padang Style (Ayam goreng Padang)

2 onions, quartered	*4 cups coconut milk*
2 cloves garlic	*1 stalk lemon grass, bruised*
2 or more fresh chillies	*Juice of half a lemon*
¼ teaspoon turmeric	*Salt, to taste*
1.5 kg (3-pound) chicken	*Oil, for frying*

Place onion, garlic, chillies and turmeric in a blender and blend on medium speed into a smooth paste. Cut the chicken into serving pieces or leave whole and split chicken in half through breast. Season chicken well with salt and the spice paste. Put aside. Pour coconut milk into a large saucepan and bring to boil, stirring continuously with down-up-over motion and cook until it thickens, for about 15 minutes. Add chicken pieces and lemon grass and continue stirring until the mixture comes to boil again. Reduce the heat to medium and cook until the chicken is tender. Add lemon juice just before finishing the cooking. Check seasoning. Lift the chicken from the pan with perforated spoon and fry until golden. However, I often prefer simply to grill the chicken lightly on both sides just before serving. This is less fussy and it accentuates flavour and aroma. Arrange chicken on a platter; pour over the sauce.

Serves 6.

Spread-eagled Spiced Chicken (Singgang ayam)

1.5 kg (3-pound) chicken
2 medium onions
2-3 cloves garlic
1 tablespoon ground chilli
1 teaspoon coriander
5 cm (2-inch) piece green ginger

¼ teaspoon turmeric
Salt, to taste
1 stalk lemon grass, bruised or
   1 teaspoon dried lemon grass
4 cups coconut milk
2 tablespoons fried onion flakes

Split chicken in half through breast only; flatten and trim, cutting off feet and neck. Combine chopped onion, garlic, ground chilli, coriander, chopped ginger and turmeric; place in blender with 2 tablespoons water. Blend on medium speed until all seasoning becomes a smooth mixture (20-25 seconds). Add salt and lemon grass. Spread half this mixture over chicken, let stand for 1 hour; reserve remaining seasonings. Take large saucepan (big enough to hold chicken), pour in coconut milk and the remaining seasonings and bring slowly to boil. Stir continuously with down-up-over motion or coconut milk will curdle. Once the mixture comes to the boil, reduce heat; cook gently until the mixture thickens (about 30 minutes), stirring constantly. Add the chicken; continue stirring while scooping sauce on to chicken until it is cooked. Remove chicken from pan, simmer sauce until it is really thick (i.e. coats a spoon), stirring occasionally. Lightly grill the chicken on both sides just before serving; this will accentuate the flavour and aroma. Arrange the chicken on a platter; pour over some of the sauce, and sprinkle with fried onion flakes.

Serves 4.

Yellow Braised Chicken (Besengek ayam)

1 plump chicken, about 1.5 kg
   (3 pounds)
5 macadamia nuts or candlenuts
5 cm (2-inch) piece green ginger,
   sliced
3 onions, chopped
3 cloves garlic
1 tablespoon ground coriander

½ teaspoon ground cummin
1 teaspoon turmeric
1 stalk lemon grass
2 tablespoons oil
2 cups coconut milk
Juice of half a lemon
Salt and freshly ground pepper,
   to taste

Cut chicken into serving pieces. Grind macadamia nuts, ginger, onions and garlic into a fine paste. Stir-fry the nut mixture together with other spices in hot oil until fragrant. Add the chicken pieces and coat well with the spices. Stir in the coconut milk and bring to boil, stirring continuously with down-up-over motion. Reduce heat and let simmer while stirring occasionally until chicken is tender and coconut milk thickens and oil seeps out. Add lemon juice and check seasoning before finishing the cooking.

Serves 6.

Stir-fried Chicken Livers with Green Beans (Sambal goreng hati dengan kacang buncis)

500 g (1 pound) chicken livers,
  cut in half
3 tablespoons peanut oil or
  margarine
4 cloves garlic, thinly sliced
2 onions, thinly sliced
2 fresh red chillies, finely sliced
  diagonally; discard seeds or
  2 capsicums, sliced in strips;
  discard seeds
5 cm (2-inch) piece green ginger,
  scraped and sliced

2 salam leaves (if available)
½ teaspoon laos (if available)
Salt, to taste
500 g (1 pound) green beans, finely
  sliced diagonally
1 cup chicken stock or 1 chicken
  stock cube dissolved in 1 cup
  hot water
½ teaspoon monosodium
  glutamate

Stir-fry chicken livers in hot oil in a large frying pan until lightly brown. Remove the livers from pan. Reduce heat, and in the remaining oil stir-fry garlic, onion, chilli, ginger, salam leaves and laos with salt until fragrant. Add beans and cook on high heat, stirring all the time for 3 minutes. Pour in chicken stock, sprinkle with monosodium glutamate. Add the stir-fried liver and cook until beans are tender.

Serves 8.

Braised Duck in Green Chilli (Gulai itik)

1 tender 1.5 kg (3-pound) duck
6 candlenuts or macadamia nuts
10 cm (4-inch) piece green ginger,
  scraped, thinly sliced
4 onions, chopped
4 tablespoons ground hot
  green chilli

3 cloves garlic, chopped
1 stalk lemon grass
1 lemon leaf
1 cup oil
Salt and pepper
1 cup water
Juice of half a lemon

Cut cleaned duck into serving pieces. Grind candlenut, green ginger, onions, chilli and garlic into a fine paste. Stir-fry the paste, lemon grass, lemon leaf in hot oil lightly for 3 minutes. Add duck pieces, salt and pepper to taste and water. Bring to boil slowly. Stir occasionally; add lemon juice. Cover pan and reduce the heat. Let simmer until the meat is tender. Check seasoning before serving. Serve with plain boiled rice and sliced cucumber, together with other dishes.

Serves 4-6.

Because of its striking pungency this dish is not recommended for beginners. However, it should be remembered that long, slow cooking effectively mellows the sharpness of chilli; thus a dish which may seem unbearably hot on the first day of preparation, has a relatively subdued but definite flavour on the second.

9 Sambal

THIS IS served as an accompaniment to most Indonesian dishes.

Yes, it is hot, and it burns the beginner's mouth so that he gasps for cold beer, iced water, sliced cucumber—anything soothing within reach—but usually he comes back again and again until he becomes an addict. Without it Indonesians find their meals dull, and Indonesians travelling abroad have been known to take a jar with them.

I suppose that, to them, a meal without *sambal* is like roast beef without mustard to an Englishman. Anyhow, if you make some and find it too hot, reduce the chilli and add a proportionately larger amount of tomato, coconut or other ingredients as suggested in the recipes, to give it body. The very hot ones I usually serve for a group of inexperienced diners in a small bowl with a tiny spoon, so that it is impossible to take too much at a time.

What does *sambal* do for a meal? It lifts up the flavour; smear a little lightly on to vegetables or a bite-sized piece of meat or fish, or fold it into a spoon of rice, then enjoy the heightened flavour and the clear sharp taste.

Coconut Fish Roe Sambal (Sambal kelapa dengan telur terubuk)

1 cup desiccated or freshly grated coconut	*4 tablespoons hot water to moisten coconut*
60 g (2 ounces) fish roe, chopped	*1 onion, grated*
¼ teaspoon turmeric	*2.5 cm (1-inch) piece ginger, scraped and grated*
2 teaspoons ground chilli	
Juice of 1 lemon	*Salt, to taste*

Mix everything together in a saucepan. Cook on low heat for 20 minutes with the lid on. Stir occasionally to prevent it from burning.

Crisp Coconut Sambal (Sambal kelapa kering)

2 onions, thinly sliced
2 fresh red chillies, finely sliced
 diagonally; discard seeds
2 tablespoons oil
2 tablespoons ground dried
 prawns

1 cup desiccated coconut
5 cm (2-inch) piece lemon grass,
 very finely sliced or 1 teaspoon
 grated lemon rind
Salt, to taste

Stir-fry onions and chillies in hot oil until soft, then add ground diced prawns, coconut, sliced lemon grass (or lemon rind) and cook on low heat until golden brown, stirring all the time. Add salt to taste. This will keep in an airtight jar for a week.

Dried Prawn Sambal I (Sambal lada udang kering I)

60 g (2 ounces) dried prawns
2 onions, thinly sliced
½ cup oil
Salt, to taste

120 g (¼ pound) fresh chillies,
 about ½ cup when ground
Juice of ½ lemon

Soak prawns in hot water until soft. Rinse and mince. Stir-fry onion in hot oil until golden; add finely ground chillies, salt to taste. Stir and reduce heat. Let simmer until chillies become tender. Add prawns and lemon juice; simmer gently another 10 minutes.

Dried Prawn Sambal II (Sambal lada udang kering II)

125 g (¼ pound) dried prawns
1 large onion
16-20 fresh red chillies
Salt, to taste

½ cup oil
½ cup very thick coconut milk
 (type I)
Juice of half a lemon

Soak prawns in boiling hot water until they are soft. Rinse and drain, then mince them. Pound the chillies and onion finely with salt. Heat oil and fry chilli mixture until soft. Add minced prawns and mix well. Then add coconut milk, stirring, and bring to boil on medium heat.

Reduce heat, allow to simmer until mixture is thick for about 30 minutes. Stir from time to time. Add lemon juice 3 minutes before finishing the cooking.

Sambal of Brown Bean Sauce (Sambal tauco)

30 g (1 ounce) dried prawns, soaked in hot water and rinsed
1 onion, thinly sliced
2 cloves garlic, chopped
5 chillies, thinly sliced diagonally, discard seeds

2.5 cm (1-inch) piece ginger, sliced
Salt, to taste
2 firm tomatoes, diced
2 tablespoons brown bean sauce

Soak prawns in hot water until soft and rinse once or twice. Chop and put aside. Stir-fry onion, garlic, chillies, ginger and salt until fragrant. Add dried prawns and stir. Lower heat and let simmer until prawns are tender. Add brown bean sauce and tomatoes in the last stage of cooking and cook on a low heat until tomatoes are soft, but not mushy.

Sambal Fried Green Chilli (Goreng sambal lada hijau)

125 g (¼ pound) green chillies
2 onions, thinly sliced
¼ cup oil
Salt, to taste

2 green tomatoes, diced
1 tin anchovy fillets in olive oil, chopped

Pound chilli into paste in a mortar or put in a blender with 2 tablespoons of water and switch on for 20 seconds on medium speed. Stir-fry onions in hot oil until golden. Add chilli and salt, stir and reduce heat. Let simmer for 2 minutes. Add diced tomatoes, chopped anchovies, oil and all. Stir and let simmer very gently for 15 minutes. Stir occasionally. This long cooking removes the bite of the chilli and blends all the flavours together. The same recipe can be prepared using red chilli instead of green chilli and ripe tomatoes instead of green ones. This sambal will keep for a week if put in the refrigerator.

Shrimp Paste Sambal (Sambal terasi)

2 tablespoons ground chilli
1 small onion
1 teaspoon shrimp paste,
   lightly grilled

Salt, to taste
Juice of half a lemon

Pound finely the chilli, onion and shrimp paste with salt to taste. Add lemon juice and blend well. Place in a bowl. This sambal is well known throughout the archipelago. However I recommend it only for addicts. If you want to make Indonesian newcomers feel at home, serve it with vegetables, plain boiled rice and with a grill. Anchovy fillets, about 2 pieces, may be substituted for shrimp paste if you wish.

Soya Sauce Sambal (Sambal kecap)

½ cup soya sauce
2 fresh chillies, cut into ringlets

1 large onion, thinly sliced
Juice of half a lemon

Combine all these ingredients and blend well. Place in a small bowl. In Indonesia it accompanies many popular dishes including fried rice. In this country it may be used to accompany grills and roast chicken served with rice. Avoid the chilli ringlets if you prefer a milder taste. The onions are particularly tasty.

Steamed Sambal, Peasant Style (Sambal lada uap)

5 fresh red chillies
1 onion, quartered
2 tomatoes

Salt, to taste
½ teaspoon shrimp paste, grilled
   lightly, or 1 anchovy fillet

Place chillies, onion and tomatoes in a bowl and steam until tender. Put in a blender with salt to taste and shrimp paste to make into a very fine paste. Or pound in a mortar.

Yields 1 small bowl.

10 Garnishes and Side-dishes

INDONESIANS are meticulous in the presentation of their dishes, particularly when they are for a formal meal, and they devote many hours to the preparation of garnishes, not only to give the food a more attractive taste, but also to add to its appearance. These garnishes are made from vegetables, eggs and meat. Among the vegetables cucumbers, tomatoes, chillies, parsley, celeriac tops, shallots, spring onions and last but not least, onions, are very popular. In fact, crisp golden fried onion flakes are sprinkled on top of many dishes, adding a finishing touch to the appearance, and providing a taste that goes with practically anything.

Garnishes from eggs are made in various ways; they are hard-boiled, quartered, or sliced thinly or thin omelettes (p. 110) are shredded into fine strips. This contributes a dash of colour as well as taste.

Meat may also be shredded for *Abon* (p. 106) which is very tasty and, as it is dark brown in colour, it is usually an effective garnish for Fried Rice, Yellow Rice, and so on. When used in combination with the shredded omelette strips and one or two vegetable garnishes, the result is a feast for the eyes as well as the palate.

The side-dishes play an equally important role and Indonesians are fond of the instant variety of flavours they provide. The crunchiness of the various kinds of *Krupuk* crackers contrasts well with the smooth texture of rice and certain vegetables. The fresh tangy taste of salad and relishes prevents the richness of creamy dishes from cloying. Of course, they are also used to make something rich or tasty, richer or tastier. In fact the variety of foods are like the instruments of an orchestra ready to play a symphony of glorious food on the taste buds. And the diner is the conductor.

How to Make Chilli Flowers

Take a red chilli, stem and all. Slice the chilli from just below the stem down to the point. Then slice each half into two in the same way. Place in iced water in the refrigerator for about an hour. The chilli strips will curve out forming a flower pattern. Such ornamental chillies can be used with parsley or water cress (the parsley as leaves, the chilli as flowers) to decorate and give colour to dishes lacking visual appeal.

How to Make Onion Brushes or Onion Flowers

Discard both the green tops and root ends of spring onions or shallots, leaving only the white stalks. Then make a number of vertical parallel cuts towards the bulb. Drop into cold iced water in the refrigerator and the ends will spring out into circular fringes. Use them to decorate crisp fried chicken, or to give colour to Soya Sauce Dip for *Saté*.

Crackers (Krupuk)

In Indonesia there are many kinds of crackers *(krupuk)* each with its own flavour. They may be made from various kinds of flour with a variety of seasonings, e.g. tapioca flour with prawn flavour *(krupuk udang)*; nuts *(krupuk emping)*; tubers *(krupuk kentang)*; beef skin *(krupuk jangat* or *cengek)*. This last one is something like crackling.

Some of them are readily available in major towns and cities in this country such as prawn-flavoured crackers, *emping* and, of course, potato crisps. Where they are not available, pappadam (Indian crackers) or Chinese prawn crackers may be good substitutes. The flavour of all crackers does not go with every dish however, and the choice of substitutes needs experience.

Prawn Crackers (Krupuk udang)

These are made in Indonesia from tapioca flour mixed with fish or shrimp paste and spices, then steamed, cut into thin slices of varying sizes, and dried. They are readily available in large stores. To cook, drop dried crackers into hot, deep oil, one or two at a time (depending on size of pan) and fry on medium heat. In about 1 minute they will have puffed up to several times their original size. Drain on absorbent paper. When cooked, they will stay crisp several days if kept in an airtight tin.

Nut Crackers (Emping)

Melinjo nuts are shelled, then carefully pounded to flatten into round shapes as soon as they have been picked. They are then put in the sun to dry. The taste is something like walnuts. They are readily available in large towns. To cook, drop nuts into hot deep oil, a handful at a time. Fry for 60 seconds on medium heat, stirring. Do not brown. Drain on absorbent paper. When cooked, they will stay crisp several days if kept in an airtight jar. If sprinkled with salt and mixed with fried onion flakes, they are an ideal accompaniment for drinks.

Potato Crisps (Krupuk kentang)

1 kg (2 pounds) potatoes   *Oil, for deep-frying*

Peel potatoes, wash and dry. Cut in thin slices. Rinse well with cold water to get rid of starch. Dry in clean cloth. Heat oil, place potato slices into a frying basket and fry for about 3 minutes or until potatoes are crisp and golden brown. Drain on absorbent paper, sprinkle with salt; toss lightly. They will stay crisp several days if kept in an airtight jar, and are used as a garnish for salad-type vegetable dishes and sometimes for *soto*.

Potato Straws

To make potato straws, follow the method above, only cut potato into strips, the size of matchsticks.

Peanut Crackers (Rempeyek)

1 cup rice flour or plain (wheat) flour
1 tablespoon cornflour
1 tablespoon ground almonds
2 cloves garlic, crushed
1 small onion, grated
1 tablespoon coriander
2 cups coconut milk
1 cup raw peanuts
Salt and pepper, to taste
Oil, for frying

Combine the two flours, ground almonds, garlic, onion and coriander in a bowl. Add coconut milk a little at a time and stir well to make a smooth batter. Add the peanuts and salt to taste and mix well. Spoon into hot oil and fry on medium heat 3 or 4 spoonfuls at a time until crisp. Since the batter is thin, it will spread evenly. Drain well on absorbent paper. Repeat the same process until the mixture is used up.

In Indonesia it is eaten by itself as a crunchy snack or served as a side-dish. Here, I serve it with drinks at informal gatherings or cocktail parties, and the platter is always quickly empty.

Crisp Shredded Beef (Abon)

500 g (1 pound) topside or skirt
   steak in a piece
2 cloves garlic, crushed
1 onion, grated
½ teaspoon laos
1 tablespoon ground coriander
½ teaspoon ground cummin

Freshly ground pepper
Salt, to taste
Juice of half a lemon or
   1 tablespoon tamarind juice
2 teaspoons brown sugar
½ cup very thick coconut milk
½ cup oil

Trim fat from meat, boil meat in a covered saucepan with 1 cup of water on low heat until tender and on the point of falling apart. Use of a pressure cooker will shorten the cooking time considerably. Take out meat and let drain. Beat meat with the flat side of a cleaver to soften and shred into strands with a fork. The results will be a heap of meat fibres. Season well with the spices and braise in coconut milk in a frying pan on medium heat until all coconut milk is absorbed, stirring all the time. When almost dry, add oil and fry until crisp. Place in a colander resting on a bowl and press to let oil drain thoroughly, separate meat fibres again into strands with a fork, then place on absorbent paper to absorb any remaining excess fat before storing it in an airtight container. This is usually used as a garnish for rice dishes, and it is very popular with children because it is tasty but not too spicy.

Cucumber Pickle (Acar bening ketimun)

5 cucumbers
3 chillies, 2 red and 1 green
   for colour effect
Salt

2 cups white vinegar (enough to
   cover cucumber pieces)
¼ cup sugar

Wash the cucumbers and cut them lengthwise into quarters. Do not peel them; discard the pulpy centres with seeds. Cut into cubes. Season cucumber cubes generously with salt. Place in the refrigerator for an hour. Rinse cucumbers in a bowl with cold water and drain well. Cut chillies into ringlets. Discard seeds. Mix the sugar and vinegar together and bring to boil; cook until the sugar dissolves. Add cucumbers, chilli ringlets and bring to boil; then remove from heat. Allow to cool and serve. If stored in a jar, this will keep for about a fortnight.

Fish Roe Relish (Anyang telur terubuk)

30 g (1 ounce) fish roe
1 tablespoon oil
2 white onions, thinly sliced

2 fresh red or green chillies, thinly sliced, diagonally; discard seeds
Juice of half a lemon

Fry fish roe in hot oil lightly, then chop. Rinse sliced onions in salt water and squeeze dry. Mix chopped fish roe well with sliced onions, chillies and lemon.

Fried Onion Flakes (Goreng bawang)

Widely used as a garnish for Indonesian dishes, they also give an interesting flavour when sprinkled over European-style soups just before serving; nice with chicken, beef, or vegetable soups. I usually make a large quantity of onion flakes at one time, than store them in an airtight jar, ready for use when required. There are two methods of making the onion flakes:

Method 1: Skin, wash, and slice onions; cut them into very thin and even slices. Heat oil enough to cover onions in frying pan; fry the onions, stirring evenly. When partly cooked, reduce heat to very low; turn onions frequently so they become evenly browned without burning. If it seems they might burn, remove from heat before they are fully browned and keep stirring. The heat of the oil should be sufficient to complete the cooking. When cooked, pour onions and oil quickly into strainer over basin. This is to avoid some of the flakes becoming overbrowned, and ensures that the onion flakes will be left crisp and dry.

Method 2: Dried onion flakes are sold at health food stores, or in packets at most grocers. For every 125 g (4 ounces) dried onion flakes, heat 1 cup oil in frying pan on medium heat. Sprinkle onion flakes into pan, stir continuously until well browned. When cooked, strain as for method 1. These dried onion flakes brown very quickly.

Hard-boiled Eggs (Telur rebus)

Place eggs in a saucepan and cover with cold water, about 3 cm (1 inch) above eggs. Bring to boil. Reduce heat. Cover and cook on low heat (just simmering) for 10-15 minutes, depending on size of eggs and whether or not they are from the refrigerator. Cool eggs immediately under cold running water to stop cooking and to make shelling easier. Shell. To slice for garnish, use an egg slicer for uniform slices and to quarter eggs, cut with a fine strong cotton. Tie the cotton to any firm anchorage in the kitchen. Place egg on palm of hand, then halve and quarter it with a quick decisive action with the taut cotton.

Meat and Potato Croquettes (Pergedel kentang dengan daging)

1.5 kg (3 pounds) potatoes
30 g (1 ounce) butter
1 small onion
2-3 cloves garlic
500 g (1 pound) minced steak
Salt and pepper, to taste

$\frac{1}{4}$ teaspoon nutmeg
4 shallots
$\frac{1}{4}$ teaspoon monosodium glutamate (optional)
2 or 3 eggs, separated
Oil, for deep-frying
Parsley, for garnishing

Cook, drain, and mash potatoes. Melt butter, add finely chopped onion and garlic. Stir-fry until they change colour, then add meat seasoned with salt, pepper, nutmeg; cook, stirring constantly. When meat is half-cooked, add very finely sliced shallots, including green tops. Remove from heat as soon as meat is cooked. In bowl combine mashed potatoes with meat mixture, monosodium glutamate, and egg yolks. Form mixture into small egg-shaped balls, refrigerate for 1 hour to firm. Beat egg whites lightly with fork in small bowl. Dip meat balls one at a time in egg whites; the egg white will form a covering skin and prevent meat balls from breaking up. Deep-fry in hot oil until golden brown. Serve hot, garnished with parsley. These can be made in advance and reheated in the oven. Made in smaller sizes, they are ideal cocktail savouries.

Serves 8-10.

Pineapple Chutney

1 small pineapple
2 red chillies, finely chopped,
  discard seeds
2 tablespoons sugar

$\frac{1}{2}$ teaspoon salt
$\frac{1}{4}$ teaspoon or 1 stick cinnamon
3 cloves

To prepare pineapple for chutney: First remove stem from pineapple by holding the pineapple in one hand and, with the other, twist the prickly top firmly until it comes off. Protect hands with gloves or cloth. Cut fruit in quarters lengthwise, then trim the hard core in the centre from each section. Peel the skin, making sure to remove all the eyes. Cut each quarter piece crosswise in 3 or 4 sections and then cut into titbits (more dainty than chunks). Place pineapple titbits in saucepan. Add chopped chilli, sugar, salt, cinnamon and cloves to the pineapple and cook for 20 minutes on medium heat, stirring occasionally. The pineapple should be soft, but not mushy. This chutney can be served hot or at room temperature to go as an accompaniment with rich creamy dishes.

Yields 2 cups or 1 serving bowl.

Roasted Coconut with Peanuts (Serundeng)

250 g ($\frac{1}{2}$ pound) raw peanuts
1 cup oil (to fry peanuts)
1 beef stock cube
$\frac{1}{4}$ cup hot water
250 g ($\frac{1}{2}$ pound) desiccated or
  freshly grated coconut
1 teaspoon sugar
1 medium onion

2 cloves garlic
1 tablespoon ground coriander
1 salam leaf
2 tablespoons oil
Salt and pepper, to taste
1 tablespoon tamarind juice
$\frac{1}{2}$ cup oil

Wash and dry peanuts, deep-fry in hot oil until crisp. Dissolve beef stock cube in hot water, pour over coconut, season with sugar. Add grated onion, grated garlic, coriander, and salam leaf, all of which have been sautéed in a little oil. Add salt and pepper to taste and tamarind juice. Mix thoroughly by hand so all spices blend with the coconut. Put into small baking dish or ovenproof dish, pour over the $\frac{1}{2}$ cup oil. Cook in moderately slow oven, for 30 minutes, stirring occasionally to keep from burning. Reduce heat to low, cook until coconut is golden brown. Remove from oven, stir in peanuts. Put in colander to drain and cool. *Serundeng* will keep in airtight jar about 2 weeks. It is very tasty if sprinkled on individual helpings of vegetable.

Savoury Coconut Balls (Rempah)

125 g (4 ounces) desiccated or
   freshly grated coconut
1 beef stock cube
¼ cup hot water
250 g (½ pound) minced steak
2 cloves garlic, crushed
2 teaspoons ground coriander

Pinch of ground cummin
1 small onion, grated
Freshly ground black pepper
Salt, to taste
1 egg
2 cups oil

Place the coconut in a bowl and moisten with ¼ cup of beef stock
made by dissolving stock cube in hot water. Add the rest of the
ingredients and mix well. Shape neatly and firmly into marble-sized balls.
Shallow-fry balls on moderate heat until brown. Drain and place on
absorbent paper.
This is usually served at traditional feasts with yellow rice together with
other side-dishes. Since these coconut balls are very rich, only a very
little should be taken with each spoonful of rice.

Savoury Potato Straws (Sambal goreng keripik kentang)

1 tablespoon oil
½ teaspoon shrimp paste
3 fresh chillies, thinly sliced
   diagonally; discard seeds

1 tablespoon brown sugar
1 tablespoon tamarind juice
3 cups potato straws
¼ cup crisp onion flakes

Heat oil and stir-fry shrimp paste and sliced chilli for 2 minutes. Add
sugar, tamarind juice and cook on low heat until sugar dissolves. Add
potato straws and onion flakes and turn a few times to coat with
seasonings. Leave to cool and keep in an airtight jar.

Thin Omelette for Garnish (Dadar telur)

Beat 3 eggs lightly with 3 tablespoons water. Season with salt and pepper
to taste. Brush frying pan with margarine; when hot, pour in enough
egg mixture to make 1 paper-thin omelette. Tip pan sideways to thin
out omelette. When cooked, roll and slice in fairly thin strips. Repeat
process with remaining egg mixture.

Sufficient to garnish 6 portions.

White Radish Relish (Acar lobak)

2 white radishes, about 250 g
(½ pound)
1 white onion, thinly sliced
crosswise
Salt

2 tablespoons white vinegar
2 fresh chillies, cut into
ringlets; discard seeds

Peel radishes and slice very thinly crosswise. Combine radish and onion slices and rub salt generously into mixture. Let stand for 10 minutes. Rinse and let drain. Add vinegar and chilli ringlets to radish mixture. Combine well together. Check seasoning and add salt if necessary. Let stand for an hour or so before serving. It goes well either with rich dishes or Western-style grills.

11 *Soto, Noodles, Laksa, Baso and Saté*

WHEN I arrived in Australia, the first two months were a period of adjustment. In the beginning I was a bit miserable and homesick, and had to keep telling myself that I had to make the best of it. What was it that troubled me the most? Mostly the difference in the style of living. I missed the people and the environment.

In Indonesia one is always conscious of being surrounded by people; the home is never empty. In contrast, life in Australia seemed silent and lonely, with each household insulated from the next.

One thing I missed was the cries, rattles and bells of the street hawkers as they plied their trade from morning to night. The chirpings of birds and hawkers' cries as they started their rounds used to be my alarm clock, blending in harmony to welcome the early morning sunshine. They sold all kinds of things, starting with fresh hot bread then as the day progressed, vegetables, fruit, fish, general household necessities, and most important from my point of view, mid-morning and evening cooked snacks.

They have their own distinctive cries and signals so that the housewife knows at once what is available outside her very door. In Indonesia these were sounds I took for granted and only missed them when the only street sound to be heard was the impersonal roar of traffic. Later I was to learn that there was the same kind of social warmth in Australia as I knew in Indonesia, and it was only the style that was different. But this is another story.

To return to the cooked snacks: *soto*, noodles, *laksa*, *baso* and *saté* are among the most popular. The hawkers selling them do their rounds with their portable stoves and wares slung on the ends of a pole carried on their shoulders or pushed in a hand cart.

I put *soto*, noodles, *laksa*, *baso* and *saté* or dishes similar to these in a separate section for they have a particular role to play in Indonesian cuisine. In addition to being useful snacks, they can also make a substantial meal. In fact a hostess can serve them to visitors for lunch with a good conscience, whereas if she served rice, she would feel she was not treating her guests with proper respect unless she served four or five dishes with it such as vegetables, chicken, eggs, *krupuk* and *sambal*.

So, the following are ideal dishes for family or close friends to whom one has said 'Do drop by and bring the children'.

SOTO

A few cookery books refer to this dish in English as 'soup'.

I looked up the word soup in a dictionary and the meaning given was 'liquid made from meat, fish or vegetables, with various added ingredients, by boiling'.

As you will discover later, after reading and trying out the recipes, *soto* is theoretically included in this category, but in practice the majority of Indonesians do not regard this dish as soup in the sense it is understood by Europeans. They have *soto* in a restaurant after the cinema, when going on a shopping expedition or for a week-end treat. Many Indonesian friends of mine serve it at bridge parties or social gatherings in much the same way as Australians serve *pizza*. Only rarely is it served as the first course of a formal meal. So, if you are in an Indonesian restaurant and you want some *soto*, do not ask for soup. You will get what you ask for but not what you want.

Chicken Soto (Soto ayam)

2 onions, chopped
3 cloves garlic, crushed
5 cm (2-inch) piece green ginger
5 candlenuts or macadamia nuts
1 teaspoon turmeric
4 or more litres water
*1 plump chicken, about 1.5 kg
  (3 pounds)*
1 stalk lemon grass
2 stalks parsley
Salt and pepper

2 chicken cubes
2 stalks celery
5 stalks shallots
¼ cabbage, finely shredded
250 g (½ pound) bean sprouts
*6 medium potaoes, boiled
  in jackets*
2-3 hard-boiled eggs
*60 g (2 ounces) shiny type
  vermicelli*

Pound onions, garlic, ginger (from which you have scraped the skin), candlenuts and turmeric into a fine paste. Bring water to the boil in a large saucepan. Add the paste, chicken, lemon grass, parsley, salt and pepper to taste. Bring back to the boil and add chicken cubes. Reduce heat and simmer chicken until tender. Add celery, cut in 2.5 cm (1-inch) pieces, 5 minutes before the end of cooking time. Skim fat from stock if you wish, take out chicken, remove bones and cut the meat into small pieces. Strain the chicken stock and keep hot. Blanch the shredded cabbage, clean and blanch the bean sprouts, peel the potatoes and cut or break into chunks, cut the eggs into quarters. Soak the vermicelli in boiling water for 10 minutes then drain well. To serve: In each heated individual serving bowl place 2 or 3 pieces of potato, 2 tablespoons vermicelli, 2 tablespoons bean sprouts, 2 tablespoons shredded cabbage, some of the chicken pieces, and on the very top, 1 or 2 quarters of hard-boiled egg. Pour hot chicken stock over the contents and sprinkle with snipped celeriac tops and onion flakes. A few drops of chilli sauce and soya sauce give a lift to the flavour. Potato crisps are a good side-dish, so have them ready at the table.

Serves 8 or more people.

Beef Soto (Soto daging)

5 candlenuts or macadamia nuts	2 stalks lemon grass
3 slices ginger	Salt and pepper
1 onion, thinly sliced	Butter, to shallow-fry beef
3 cloves garlic, thinly sliced	2 beef stock cubes
1 tablespoon butter	1 tablespoon soya sauce
3 litres water	1 teaspoon monosodium
¼ teaspoon turmeric	glutamate
750 g (1½ pounds) chuck steak	

GARNISH

60 g (2 ounces) shiny Chinese vermicelli (soun)	Snipped celeriac tops or parsley ½ cup onion flakes

Grind nuts, ginger into a smooth paste. Put aside. Stir-fry onion and garlic in hot butter until soft. Add water, nut paste, turmeric, meat, lemon grass with salt and pepper. Bring to boil, then simmer until meat is tender. Take out the meat and cut up into 1 cm (½-inch) cubes. Lightly fry in butter, then return meat cubes to the stock. Add beef, stock cubes, soya sauce and monosodium glutamate. Check seasonings. To serve: Pour broth, beef and all, into a large serving bowl or tureen and place on the table, together with garnishes heaped decoratively on a platter (e.g. vermicelli in the centre with onion flakes and snipped celeriac tops on either side) for diners to help themselves. Beef soto is usually accompanied with potato balls; it must be served hot.

Serves 6.

Meat and Potato Croquettes
(Pergedel kentang dengan
daging) before frying

Potato Balls (Pergedel kentang)

750 g (1½ pounds) potatoes,
    boiled in jackets
2 eggs, separated
1 shallot, thinly sliced
1 tablespoon snipped celeriac
    top or parsley

Salt and pepper, to taste
½ teaspoon nutmeg
Oil, for frying

Peel and mash potatoes until smooth. In a bowl combine mashed potatoes with egg yolks, finely sliced shallot including green top, snipped celeriac top or snipped parsley. Season with salt, pepper and nutmeg. Form mixture into small egg-shaped balls and refrigerate for 1 hour to firm. Beat egg white lightly with a fork in a small bowl. Dip potato balls one at a time in egg white and deep-fry in hot oil until golden brown. These can be made in advance and reheated in oven.

Tripe Soto (Soto babat)

500 g (1 pound) tripe, parboiled
    (discard broth)
4 chicken stock cubes
2 litres water
4 cloves garlic, finely sliced
7 cm (3-inch) piece green ginger,
    sliced
1 tablespoon butter
Salt and pepper, to taste
1 stalk lemon grass

2 Chinese radishes, peeled and
    diced
3 stalks shallots
125 g (¼ pound) bean sprouts,
    scalded
¼ cup fried onion flakes
1 tablespoon snipped celeriac tops
125 g (4 ounces) dried white soya
    beans, soaked overnight
2 cups oil
Sambal (see below)

Cut tripe into bite-sized pieces. Put aside. Stir-fry garlic and ginger in hot butter in large saucepan until fragrant. Add tripe pieces, water, chicken stock cubes, lemon grass, salt and pepper to taste. Bring to boil and then let simmer until tripe is tender. Add diced Chinese radishes and cook until tender. Add shallots cut up in pieces 2.5 cm (1-inch) long, leaves also, 2 minutes before finishing the cooking. Check seasoning. Serve hot in the following way. To prepare soya bean garnish: Parboil and drain white soya beans. Fry beans in hot oil until crisp, stirring all the time. Place in colander to drain oil and then place on absorbent paper to absorb any remaining excess fat. To serve: Spoon hot soto with some bean sprouts into individual bowls about ¾ full. Add fried soya beans, sprinkle fried onion flakes and snipped celeriac tops on top. Let diners help themselves with the sambal. This can be eaten by itself or

Chicken Soto with garnishes,
ready for serving

with boiled plain rice. Sometimes broken up potato crisps are also sprinkled on top.

SAMBAL

2 fresh red chillies or
   1 teaspoon sambal oelek
3 macadamia nuts

Salt, to taste
Juice of 1 lemon

Pound all ingredients together into a smooth paste. Add 2 tablespoons tripe stock to moisten sambal. Place in a bowl together with a tiny serving spoon.

Serves 4-6.

Parboiled Egg Noodles (Merebus mie)

8 cups water
1 teaspoon salt

375 g (12 ounces) noodles

Bring water to boil vigorously in a large saucepan. Add salt, then gradually add noodles, making sure the water remains boiling. From time to time stir noodles to loosen so that they cook evenly. Cooking time is usually about 5-7 minutes. Test for doneness by biting a single strand. The outside should be tender while the inside is still firm. If overcooked, the noodles will be mushy. Drain noodles in colander, rinse with cold water to prevent their continuing to cook in their own heat. This rinsing also removes excess starch, and stops the noodles from sticking to each other. Boiled noodles will keep for several days if drained well, tossed in a small quantity of oil (1 tablespoon for 375 g [12 ounces]) and kept in refrigerator in a plastic bag or airtight container.

Noodles in Broth (Mie kuah)

185 g (6 ounces) parboiled egg
  .noodles
2 cloves garlic, thinly sliced
1 onion, thinly sliced
1 tablespoon oil or margarine
7 cups water
2 slices fresh ginger
500 g (1 pound) chicken breasts
Salt and freshly ground pepper

4 cabbage leaves, discard core;
  shredded
1 cup bean sprouts, cleaned
2 shallots or spring onions,
  including green tops
¼ teaspoon monosodium glutamate
  (optional)
¼ cup snipped celeriac top
¼ cup fried onion flakes

Stir-fry garlic and onion slices in oil in a large saucepan until soft. Add water, ginger, chicken breast, salt and pepper to taste and bring to boil. Reduce heat, cook chicken until tender. Take out chicken; bone and shred when cool. Add shredded cabbage and bean sprouts, shallots or spring onion cut in 1 cm (½-inch) pieces to stock and cook for 2 minutes. Return chicken pieces to saucepan to heat through. Add monosodium glutamate. Check seasoning. Place noodles in a large tureen or individual bowls. Pour over hot broth, garnish with snipped celeriac tops and fried onion flakes and serve.

Serves 4-6.

Stir-fried Beef and Vegetables on Noodles (Mie goreng pakai daging)

500 g (1 pound) round steak
2 onions, thinly sliced
2 cloves garlic, crushed
2.5 cm (1-inch) piece green ginger, scraped and sliced
Salt and pepper, to taste
Oil or margarine, for frying

2 stalks celery, sliced 1 cm (½-inch) thick, diagonally
60 g (2 ounces) mushrooms, sliced uniformly
1 beef stock cube, crumbled
250 g (½ pound) bean sprouts
2 tablespoons soya sauce
2 stalks spring onions, thinly sliced

Pound meat lightly with back of chopper to make it tender; slice into strips 5 cm (2 inches) long and ½ cm (¼ inch) wide. Stir-fry onion slices, garlic and ginger with salt in hot oil or margarine until soft. Add sliced beef and stir-fry until brown and tender. Take out meat. Add more oil, heat and stir-fry sliced celery and mushrooms with crumbled beef stock cube for 3 minutes before adding bean sprouts and soya sauce with pepper to taste. If canned bean sprouts are used, rinse and drain well. Stir well and cook assorted vegetables for another 2 minutes. Put beef back into vegetable mixture just to heat through. Check seasoning. Keep hot while you prepare noodles for serving.

185 g (6 ounces) egg noodles
8 cups water

1 teaspoon salt
1½ tablespoons butter

Drop noodles in boiling salted water and when they begin to soften, separate with a fork. Drain well, rinse under running water. Mix lightly with butter to stop it from sticking together. Heat in the oven for 10 minutes, loosely covered with aluminium foil. Place hot buttered noodles on a platter as base and border, and pile up the meat and vegetable mixture in the middle.

Serves 4-6.

Stir-fried Noodles (Mie goreng)

3 medium onions
3 cloves garlic
1 small chicken breast
2 pieces fillet steak
5 shallots
2 eggs
375 g (¾ pound) dried noodles
3 tablespoons margarine or oil

125 g (4 ounces) prawns
2 tablespoons soya sauce
½ cup chicken stock
1 cup snow peas, cabbage or
    bean sprouts
Salt and pepper, to taste
¼ cup fried, crisp onion flakes

Slice onions thinly, chop garlic finely. Bone, cut chicken into small pieces, slice steak into thin strips. Cut shallots into 2.5 cm (1-inch) pieces. Use the 2 eggs to make thin omelettes. Drop noodles into large saucepan of boiling salted water, cook 5 minutes. Rinse with cold water, drain; set aside. Stir-fry the onions and garlic in melted margarine until brown. Add steak, chicken pieces, prawns, soya sauce, stock; cook 10 minutes. Add shallots and snow peas or cabbage or bean sprouts; cook until vegetables are tender. Add noodles to mixture, mix thoroughly. Taste for seasoning. Arrange on platter, garnish with onion flakes and omelettes sliced into thin strips.

Serves 5.

Beef Balls with Noodles (Mie rebus)

STAGE I
375 g (12 ounces) parboiled egg noodles (p. 116)

STAGE II
2 onions, grated
2 cloves garlic, crushed
1 tablespoon oil or margarine
750 g (1½ pounds) minced topside
4 slices slightly stale bread, diced

1 egg, beaten lightly
½ teaspoon nutmeg
Salt and pepper, to taste

Sauté onions and garlic in hot oil until fragrant. Combine meat, bread, sautéed onion and garlic, egg, nutmeg, salt and pepper. When well mixed, form into 18 firm round balls. Put aside.

STAGE III

1 onion, thinly sliced	*2.5 cm (1-inch) piece green ginger,*
2 cloves garlic, crushed	*scraped and bruised*
1 tablespoon oil or margarine	*4 shallots or spring onions, sliced*
4 cups water	*4 stalks celery, uniformly sliced*
3 chicken stock cubes	*4 cabbage leaves, finely shredded*

Sauté onion and garlic in oil until fragrant. Add water, crumbled chicken stock cubes, ginger and bring to boil. Place meatballs gently into the broth and allow to return to boil; keep on medium heat until the meat is cooked. Check seasoning. Add vegetables 5-7 minutes before the cooking time is finished. The vegetables should be crunchy, but not underdone. Serve hot in individual bowls by placing in each one-sixth of the noodles, 3 meatballs and some vegetables; top up each bowl with broth. Sprinkle with snipped celeriac leaves or parsley, if you wish.

Serves 6.

To Parboil Rice Sticks (Merebus beehoon)

Wash rice sticks in cold water and place in a colander. Rest the colander on top of a large saucepan. Pour boiling water over rice sticks and stir well. Let drain. Scald again with the same hot water to soften if necessary, drain. Rice sticks should be cooked through but firm. To save time, the rice sticks may be dropped for 2 minutes in a pan of boiling water, but care is necessary, otherwise they may become mushy. Rice sticks, rice noodles, rice vermicelli, *laksa, beehoon* are in fact the same thing. Not to be confused with the shiny type vermicelli that is called in Indonesian *soun*.

Rice Sticks with Tasty Coconut Milk (Laksa)

2 onions, sliced	*1 teaspoon turmeric powder*
2 cloves garlic, sliced	*2 tablespoons oil*
5 cm (2-inch) piece green ginger,	*8 cups coconut milk*
scraped and sliced	*4 chicken stock cubes*
4 candlenuts or macadamia nuts	*Salt, to taste*
2 chillies	*500 g (1 pound) green prawns,*
1 tablespoon coriander powder	*shelled, deveined*
½ teaspoon ground cummin seed	*250 g (½ pound) rice sticks,*
2 stalks lemon grass, whole, bruised	*parboiled*

250 g (½ pound) bean sprouts,
   cleaned, scalded and drained
3 hard-boiled eggs, quartered

2 tablespoons crisp onion flakes
¼ cup snipped celeriac tops

Place onion, garlic, ginger, nuts, chilli in a blender and blend with 2 tablespoons water into a smooth paste. Stir-fry paste, coriander, caraway seed, lemon grass and turmeric in hot oil until fragrant. Add coconut milk, crumbled chicken stock cubes, salt to taste, and bring to boil, stirring all the time with down-up-over motion. Add prawns and cook on medium heat stirring all the time until the prawns are tender. Check seasoning. Serve hot in individual bowls. Place 2 or more tablespoons of parboiled rice sticks in each bowl; add some bean sprouts, pour over hot gravy and pieces of prawn. Garnish with 2 quartered hard-boiled eggs, onion flakes and snipped celeriac leaves or parsley.

Serves 6.

Fish Baso (Baso ikan)

FISH BALLS

1 shallot
2.5 cm (1-inch) piece green ginger
½ cup water
½ teaspoon salt

500 g (1 pound) fish fillets
1 egg white
1 teaspoon cornflour

BROTH

125 g (4 ounces) vermicelli
   (rice sticks; p. 119)
2 cloves garlic, thinly sliced
1 onion, thinly sliced
2 tablespoons oil or margarine
1 chicken breast, boned and cut
   into small pieces
5 cups chicken stock
Salt and freshly ground pepper,
   to taste

2 carrots, peeled, sliced
   diagonally
4 cabbage leaves, coarsely
   shredded
¼ teaspoon monosodium
   glutamate (optional)
¼ cup snipped celeriac tops
¼ cup fried onion flakes

Mince shallot stalk and ginger. Add to the water in a small bowl and mix well. Strain, discarding residue, and put in blender. Add salt. Cut fish fillets in 2 cm (½-1 inch) cubes, add to liquid in blender. Blend for about 60 seconds at low speed or until there is a fine smooth paste. Transfer to a bowl. Beat egg white until stiff and fold into fish together with cornflour. Form fish mixture into walnut-sized balls and place in cold salted water until ready to cook. If the fish mixture is too soft to form into balls, take a handful of the mixture and squeeze out through a clenched first between thumb and forefinger in walnut-sized balls, cutting with a spoon and letting drop into cold salted water. But if the mixture is of a drier consistency, shape the fishballs between the palms of the hands. Moisten the hands first.

Scald the rice vermicelli with hot water until soft. Stir-fry garlic and sliced onion until soft. Add chicken pieces and fry until tender. Take out chicken and put aside. Add chicken stock, salt and pepper to taste and bring to boil. Add carrot slices and cook till tender. Take fishballs from salted cold water with a perforated spoon and place in boiling broth. Cook until done (3 to 5 minutes). Add shredded cabbage and chicken pieces and cook for another 2 minutes. Add monosodium glutamate. Check seasoning. Serve hot. Place drained vermicelli in a serving bowl (or tureen). Pour broth, vegetables and all over it. Sprinkle with snipped celeriac tops and fried onion flakes just before serving. Let diners help themselves to *baso*.

Yields 12 fish balls; serves 4.

SATE

Saté is sold by hawkers in all kinds of places and at any time of the day. Favourite spots for the hawkers are railway stations, bus terminals, market places, street corners and, of course, holiday resorts.

In some districts *saté*-making is a family business which has developed into a fine art. The details of the sauce recipes are jealously guarded and handed down from father to son who take care to keep up the family reputation. I remember a famous *saté* vendor in my home town called Mak Ajaik who, when I was a little girl, already had grey hair. As far as I know, the business is still going strong under the same name. Such places are popular and throngs of people visit them. *Saté* is served with *lontong* (p. 27) or *ketupat* (p. 28) and when eaten with either of these, can form quite a substantial snack. It is all the more appetising because it is cooked in front of the customer. I sometimes serve it for a barbecue, when it is fun for friends to help; in fact, the beauty of it is that the host need only prepare the skewered meat, the sauces and the fire, and then watch the food disappear. *Saté* goes well with green salad or coleslaw and bread rolls. But if you want to go completely Indonesian, serve it with Fried Rice (p. 23), Yellow Rice (p. 22), Gado-gado (p. 42) or Pecal (p. 42) with boiled rice as a base. I find dainty chicken *saté* an ideal accompaniment for drinks at a special cocktail party.

There are many types of skewers available, metal or wood, thick or thin. I prefer to avoid the metal ones, because they retain heat longer and the diner may burn his lips. My favourite is bamboo; light but strong, they can easily be cut into small sections with only three or four dainty pieces of meat on each to serve with drinks.

Europeans sometimes find eating *saté* a problem. The most practical way is to hold the stick in the right hand, parallel to the lips, and detach the pieces of meat from the left, one by one, with the teeth.

Peanut Sauce

Ground peanuts are an important ingredient in several sauces. In Indonesia, fresh peanuts are fried or roasted, then skinned and ground into a paste to be mixed with other ingredients as appropriate for the sauce to be prepared. Among these sauces are those for *Saté*, Bean Curd, *Gado-gado* and *Pecal*.

Hawkers selling Fried Soya Bean Curd (p. 125) sometimes prepare the sauce in front of their customers, grinding the peanuts with a grinding stone. Practice has made their fingers nimble and they do it very quickly. Busy housewives may prefer to economise on time and effort by using crunchy peanut butter in the same quantity as the ground roasted peanuts. The taste is not as good, however.

Savoury Beef Saté (Saté bumbu)

500 g (1 pound) rump steak
1 onion, quartered
2 cloves garlic
2 chillies or 1 teaspoon
   sambal oelek
2 macadamia nuts
1 5 cm (2-inch) piece green ginger, sliced
1 teaspoon ground coriander

½ teaspoon turmeric
1 tablespoon oil
¼ teaspoon brown sugar
   (optional)
1 salam leaf (if available)
1 lemon leaf
Salt, to taste

Cut the meat into 2 cm (¾-inch) cubes. Put aside. Grind onion, garlic, chillies, macadamia nuts and ginger into a smooth paste. Stir-fry the nut paste together with coriander and turmeric in hot oil for 2 minutes. Add brown sugar, meat, salam leaf, lemon leaf and salt to taste; coat well with the spices. Continue cooking while turning meat constantly for another 5 minutes. Leave to cool. Then thread meat cubes on skewers, 4 or 5 cubes on each, and grill over charcoal fire or under the griller, basting with the remaining spice mixture. Unlike other types of *saté*, this one does not have an accompanying sauce.
Serves 4.

Skewered Lamb Grill (Saté kambing)

Cut 750 g (1½ pounds) lean lamb into 2 cm (¾-inch) cubes, thread on to thin bamboo skewers. Place 4-6 cubes on each skewer. There should be enough meat cubes for about 20 skewers. Grill until meat is done, turning several times. Serve hot with either of the following *saté* sauces.

SOYA SAUCE

2 shallots (discard the tops)
4 tablespoons soya sauce
2 cloves garlic, chopped

1 teaspoon ground chilli
2 tablespoons lemon juice

Slice shallots thinly crosswise; combine with remaining ingredients in oblong dish. This shape is an easy one in which to dip the *saté* sticks.

PEANUT SAUCE

1 small onion
2 cloves garlic, chopped
1 tablespoon oil
½ teaspoon ground chilli
1 cup water

½ cup peanut butter
½ teaspoon sugar
1 tablespoon soya sauce
1 tablespoon lemon juice

Thinly slice onion. Sauté onion and garlic in oil until transparent; add ground chilli. Reduce heat, stir well. Add water, then peanut butter and sugar; bring slowly to boil. Continue stirring until mixture becomes smooth. Remove from the heat. Season with soya sauce and lemon juice. Taste; add a little salt if necessary.

Minced Lamb Saté (Magbub)

1 cup oil
2 brown onions, thinly sliced
3 cloves garlic
1 tablespoon coriander seeds
1 tablespoon tamarind juice
1 teaspoon brown sugar

2 tablespoons very thick coconut
* milk (type I) or 2 tablespoons*
* top of milk*
500 g (1 pound) boned leg of lamb,
* minced, fat and all*

Heat oil in a frying pan and fry onion slices and garlic until lightly brown. Drain and put aside. Dry-fry coriander for 2 minutes, stirring constantly; grind to a powder in a blender on low speed. Add onion, tamarind juice, brown sugar, coconut milk (or milk) and salt to taste and blend for 10 seconds. Combine the coriander mixture with lamb and mix well. Divide mixture into 10 portions and shape each like a round log. Wrap each log of meat neatly in foil and grill over charcoal or under the griller for about 6 minutes, turn and grill 6 minutes longer until meat is done. Unwrap and serve with your favourite green salad.

Serves 5.

Skewered Chicken Grill (Saté ayam)

500 g (1 pound) chicken breasts
2 cloves garlic, thinly sliced
2 tablespoons soya sauce

2 tablespoons water
Oil, margarine or butter,
    to baste chicken

Cut boned chicken breasts into 2 cm ($\frac{3}{4}$-inch) cubes. Thread 5-6 cubes on to each bamboo skewer. Mix garlic, soya sauce and water. Dip the threaded chicken pieces into this mixture and grill until meat is done, basting with oil, margarine or butter several times to prevent drying out; turn several times. Do not overcook. Serve hot with Peanut Sauce (below).

SAUCE

1 small onion, thinly sliced
1 tablespoon oil or margarine
1 cup water
4 tablespoons crunchy peanut
    butter

$\frac{1}{2}$ teaspoon ground chilli
Pinch salt
$\frac{1}{2}$ teaspoon sugar
2 teaspoons soya sauce
Juice of half a lemon

Stir-fry onion in hot oil until soft. Add water, peanut butter, ground chilli, salt and sugar and stir well. Cook over low heat stirring constantly until it thickens. Stir in soya sauce and lemon juice. Check seasoning. Pour sauce over saté or serve as a dip.

Yields 15 skewers.

Skewered Ox Heart (Saté Padang)

1 ox heart, about 750 g (1$\frac{1}{2}$ pounds)
 · after trimming
3 cloves garlic
2 onions
5 cm (2-inch) piece green ginger,
    scraped
1 tablespoon ground chilli
1 teaspoon turmeric
$\frac{1}{2}$ teaspoon laos

1 tablespoon ground coriander
$\frac{1}{4}$ teaspoon ground cummin seeds
Salt, to taste
1 stalk lemon grass
1 lemon leaf
2 tablespoons rice flour
2 dozen thin bamboo skewers

Remove fat and vessels from heart, cut into 1.5 cm (2-inch) cubes. Place in large saucepan, add enough water to cover heart. Place all ingredients in a blender except lemon grass, lemon leaf and rice flour. Add 2 tablespoons of water and blend on medium speed until all seasonings become a smooth paste (30-40 seconds). Add the paste to the saucepan containing the heart and water. Bring heart to boil and then let simmer for $1\frac{1}{2}$ hours until tender. Take out heart cubes and reserve broth. Place 5-6 cubes of heart on each skewer to be grilled in due course. Meanwhile make rice flour into a thin paste by mixing with a little water. Stir the paste into broth and cook until thickened. Check seasoning, keep hot. Grill heart on skewers until light brown, turning several times. Baste occasionally with animal fat or oil to prevent it from drying out. Pour hot thick broth on top. Serve 3 or 4 skewers per person. This is usually served with *Ketupat* (boiled compressed rice).

Serves 4 or more.

Grilled Skewered Prawns (Saté udang)

2 cloves garlic, crushed
$\frac{1}{4}$ teaspoon finely ground chilli
$\frac{1}{4}$ teaspoon shrimp paste
2 tablespoons oil
10 macadamia nuts, ground
  or ground almonds

$\frac{1}{4}$ teaspoon paprika
Juice of 1 lemon
Salt, to taste
16 large green prawns, shelled
  and deveined

Stir-fry garlic, ground chilli and crumbled shrimp paste in hot oil for 1 minute. Remove pan from stove for further cooking is not necessary. Add to garlic mixture ground macadamia nuts, season with paprika, lemon juice and salt to taste. Mix until well blended. Place prawns in nut mixture to coat, then thread on to skewers, 4 prawns to each skewer. Spread half of the remaining paste on to one side of the prawns, then grill that side for 4-5 minutes; spread the other half of the paste on the uncooked side of the prawns, then turn and grill another 4-5 minutes.

Serves 4.

Fried Soya Bean Curd with Sauce (Goreng tahu dengan sambal kecap)

6 soya bean curds
250 g ($\frac{1}{2}$ pound) bean sprouts

2 stalks celery
2 tablespoons fried onion flakes

SAUCE

1 onion, thinly sliced
2 cloves garlic, finely chopped
½ teaspoon ground chilli or
* 1 chilli, very finely sliced,*
* discard seeds*
2 tablespoons oil

1 cup water
4 tablespoons peanut butter
½ cup soya sauce
Juice of half a lemon
½ teaspoon sugar

Deep-fry soya bean curds until they are golden brown, turning them once. Drain on absorbent paper before cutting up into 2.5 cm (1-inch) cubes. Put aside. Blanch bean sprouts; cut celery stems into 2.5 cm (1-inch) slices, chop leaves very finely and blanch celery stems. Drain well. Arrange soya bean curd cubes, blanched bean sprouts and blanched celery stems on a platter. Sprinkle chopped celery leaves (or snipped celeriac tops) and onion flakes on top.

Sauce: Sauté onion, garlic and chilli lightly together in oil. Add water, peanut butter, soya sauce, lemon juice and sugar to onion mixture. Stir and bring slowly to the boil. Pour over the fried bean curds and blanched vegetables just before serving. Indonesians do serve this with rice, but it is also delicious by itself.

Serves 4 persons.

12 *Snacks and Sweetmeats*

RAMADHAN, the ninth month of the Muslim year is a fasting month, and in Muslim communities neither food nor drink is taken, cigarettes, pipes or cigars smoked, from the time it is light enough to distinguish a white thread from a black one until the sun has set. In the tropics this entails a fast of between thirteen and fourteen hours.

The evening breaking of the fast, after the long hot day refraining from eating and drinking, is certainly an important social event. Desserts generally play little part in the everyday menu which usually concludes with fresh tropical fruit, but during the fasting month, the skill of the housewife in preparing desserts of various kinds and light and delicate sweetmeats comes into its own. Some people prefer to break their fast with a sweet dish first, before performing the sunset prayers, then follow with a hearty dinner which usually ends with a few sweets.

During the fasting month the schools are shut, the children at home, people come home from great distances, reunions are planned and expected. All come and go to suit themselves which involves a lot of visiting and entertaining and, of course, cooking. Along with the increased atmosphere of religious devotion goes almost instinctively the preparation of feasts. Religion and custom go hand in hand. Devoted and thoughtful wives will fulfil their obligations at least once in that month by bringing four or five kinds of delicacies placed decoratively on copper trays *(dulang)* to their mothers-in-law and senior members of the family as a sign of respect. It is not uncommon for a well-liked head of a district to receive from well-wishers five or six trays of sweetmeats a day during the fasting period. Many of these will be taken to the mosque for the worshippers.

For some of the young folk night is turned into day. After the evening meal they may gather at the mosque to recite Qur'an, then on returning home, the menfolk, sometimes with friends, are greeted with sweetmeats again. The last meal of the night is about 2 a.m., after which the energetic young men spend the rest of the night roaming the town or visiting their friends and enjoying such delights until dawn creeps into the sky and food and drink are again forbidden. So, after the dawn prayer, the young men in town retire to sleep until late in the morning.

For this section I have chosen some sweets and delicacies that can be served for desserts or for morning coffee or afternoon tea.

Garlic-flavoured Peanuts (Kacang bawang)

500 g (1 pound) raw shelled
  peanuts
6 cloves garlic, finely pounded
  or grated
Salt, to taste

$\frac{1}{2}$ cup crisp fried onion flakes
$\frac{1}{4}$ cup finely snipped celeriac tops
  or snipped parsley (fried)
2 cups oil

Pour boiling water over peanuts to blanch. Let stand 5-10 minutes. Drain. Remove and discard pinkish inner skin. Season peanuts generously with garlic and salt. Fry peanuts in hot oil until golden, stirring all the time. An alternative method is to heat oil in a frypan and dip nuts, in a fine mesh frying basket, into it. Keep peanuts moving or they will burn.) Repeat the process for the remaining peanuts. Drain thoroughly on absorbent paper. Stir-fry snipped celeriac tops on low heat until crisp but not burnt. Drain and place on absorbent paper. Mix together peanuts, crisp onion flakes and celeriac tops in a bowl. When cool, store in an airtight container. Serve with drinks. The garnish is supposed to be eaten too as it complements the flavour of the nuts.

In Indonesia this is very popular among students who munch it by the handful while doing their homework (it is supposed to increase brain power!). At boarding school two or three tins a month are eagerly expected from home.

Flaming Banana Fan

4 large bananas
1 egg white, beaten lightly
90 g (3 ounces) butter
4 tablespoons brown sugar
Juice of 3 oranges

$\frac{1}{4}$ teaspoon grated nutmeg
$\frac{1}{4}$ teaspoon ground cinnamon
4 tablespoons rum
$\frac{1}{4}$ litre cream, whipped, or the same
  quantity of vanilla ice cream

Cut bananas in two, crosswise, and peel. Make three or four parallel cuts with a very sharp knife in each half down towards the end of banana. Spread gently into a form of a fan. Dip in egg white. Heat butter in heatproof serving dish. Fry banana fans, sprinkle with sugar until brown on both sides. Be careful not to break bananas. Pour orange juice flavoured with nutmeg and cinnamon over browned banana fans; cook and let simmer for about 3 minutes. Remove from heat, sprinkle with rum and ignite. Serve with whipped cream. It is fun to prepare this for dessert in front of diners when everything is prepared beforehand. Even husbands enjoy doing it.

Serves 4.

Banana Fritters (Pisang goreng)

125 g (4 ounces) fritter batter   *Oil, for deep-frying*
5 bananas (not over-ripe)   *Icing sugar*

Make fritter batter as in the following recipe. Peel and cut bananas in two crosswise. Make 2 or 3 parallel cuts in each half, down towards the end of the banana. Spread gently into a form of a fan. Dip banana pieces in batter and deep-fry until golden. Drain on absorbent paper. Serve hot as dessert or for afternoon tea, sprinkled with icing sugar. Place, piled high, on a paper doily.

Fritter Batter (Adonan kulit penggoreng)

125 g (4 ounces) flour   *1 cup lukewarm water*
Pinch of salt   *1 egg white*

Place flour and salt in a basin. Make a well in the middle. Add water, a little at a time and with the back of a wooden spoon, stir in flour gradually. Beat into a smooth batter. Lightly fold in stiffly beaten egg white just before using.

This batter is ideal for all kinds of fruit fritters, such as pineapple, dates, prunes and so on.

Stuffed Date Fritters (Kurma dengan amandel)

250 g (½ pound) loose dates, stoned   *Make half of the quantity of*
60 g (2 ounces) blanched almonds   *batter in preceding recipe*
Oil, for deep-frying

Stuff each date with an almond. Dip into batter and deep-fry in hot oil until brown. Drain on absorbent paper. These can be made in advance. Serve with coffee.

I suppose you are wondering whether dates grow in Indonesia. No, they do not. But during the fasting month there are dates imported from the Middle East readily available in every market. This is a time when Indonesians eat dates as a matter of course, and this is one of the many little touches by which they associate themselves with the Middle East, the heartland of Islam.

Batter for Pancakes (Adonan pannekoek)

125 g (4 ounces) flour   2 eggs
Pinch of salt   2 cups milk

Sift flour with salt into a bowl, make a well; add eggs. Stir the flour in gradually from the sides. Add the milk a little at a time and beat well to remove all lumps and make the batter light and smooth. Let stand, covered for 1 or 2 hours.

Serves 4.

This is the basic recipe. Various flavours can be added as below.

Pancakes (Pannekoek)

Pancake batter   Honey
½ teaspoon vanilla   1 lemon
2 tablespoons butter

Stir vanilla into batter. Heat a little butter in an omelette pan until it smokes and goes brown. Smear over all the surface and wipe quite dry with absorbent paper. Again put a little butter in the pan and allow to melt. Pour batter in the pan and tilt pan about to cover surface evenly. Cook quickly till set and slightly brown. Loosen edges and turn over pancake with a knife; lightly brown the other side. Repeat process until the mixture is used up. Pile the pancakes on a plate after brushing the top of each one with butter. Serve hot with honey and lemon.

Skewered Chicken Grill (Saté ayam) marinating, and Skewered Lamb Grill before cooking, with peanut sauce and soya sauce

Serves 4.

Banana Pancakes *(Pannekoek pisang)*

2 eggs	*Coconut. milk or milk*
1 tablespoon sugar	*5 bananas*
125 g (4 ounces) self-raising flour	*Oil, for frying*
¼ teaspoon salt	*Sugar and lemon juice to*
1 teaspoon baking powder	*sprinkle on pancakes*

Beat eggs and sugar until light. Sift flour, salt and baking powder and fold into beaten eggs alternately with coconut milk or milk. Add mashed banana and mix well. Fry in hot oil till slightly brown. Loosen edges and turn over pancake; lightly brown the other side. Repeat process until the mixture is used up. Serve hot, sprinkled with sugar and a few drops of lemon or lime juice.

Serves 4.

Serve this dish for a change as a week-end breakfast.

Glutinous Rice with Sweet and Creamy Sauce *(Nasi tuai)*

2 cups glutinous rice	*1 cup very thick coconut milk*
2½ cups water	*(type I)*
Pinch of salt	

Wash rice under cold water until the water runs clear. Place rice in a saucepan with 2½ cups water and salt. Bring to boil. Stir briefly with a clean handle of a wooden spoon. Allow to cook until the water has all been absorbed. Stir in the coconut milk; mix thoroughly and place rice in a steamer to steam. Steam for about 15-20 minutes or until rice is tender. Serve with creamy sauce below.

SAUCE

60 g (2 ounces) brown sugar,	*1 piece cinnamon stick*
broken in very small pieces	*Pinch of salt*
2 cups very thick coconut milk	
(type I)	

Place all ingredients in a saucepan and slowly bring to the boil, stirring all the time. Let simmer for 3 minutes. Strain through a piece of muslin. To serve, pour sauce over individual helpings.

Serves 4.

Skewered Lamb Grill *(Saté kambing)* cooked on charcoal

This is a very filling sweet. It is usually served during harvesting to the helping hands together with morning coffee.

Wrapped Stuffed Glutinous Rice (Lemper ayam)

2 cups glutinous rice
2½ cups coconut milk
1 medium onion
2 cloves garlic
Candlenuts
½ teaspoon coriander
¼ teaspoon cummin
Butter

⅛ teaspoon monosodium
  glutamate
1 large chicken breast, boned
  and finely shredded
Salt and pepper, to taste
¼ teaspoon grated lemon rind
Banana leaves or silver foil

Soak glutinous rice for two hours. Drain well and cook rice in 2¼ cups coconut milk and salt in the usual way (absorption method). Put aside. Stuffing: Grind onion, garlic, candlenuts to a paste. Stir-fry the paste together with coriander and cummin in hot butter for two minutes. Add chicken, salt and pepper and keep stirring. Add the remaining ¼ cup coconut milk, monosodium glutamate and lemon rind; cook until chicken is tender and the mixture is fairly dry. Divide rice into equal portions (about 15 or more). Stuff each with 1 tablespoon of the chicken mixture, wrap in silver foil or banana leaf and fold securely in cylindrical form. If banana leaf is used hold it in place with toothpicks. Place in moderate oven for 15-20 minutes, or grill over a charcoal fire.

Serves 10.

In Indonesia *lemper* is served between meals as a snack. In Australia I serve it for afternoon tea parties together with other delicacies, or at a reception.

Fermented Glutinous Rice (Tapai pulut)

3 cups glutinous rice (pulut)
  washed and drained

3 cups water
2 level teaspoons powdered ragi

Wash rice under cold water until the water runs clear. Place rice in a saucepan with 3 cups water. Bring to boil. Stir with a clean handle of a wooden spoon. Then reduce heat to very low and cook covered until all the liquid is absorbed (about 15 minutes). Do not remove lid. Or, better still, use an automatic rice cooker to cook the rice. Spread the cooked rice on a platter to cool a little. Pass the *ragi* through a fine wire sieve. Measure two level teaspoons of *ragi*, sprinkle it on the rice and mix *ragi* and rice well. Place in a plastic container with a tight cover and place container in a warm part of the house, covered with warm rugs; leave for 36 hours to ferment. After fermentation is complete, chill in refrigerator before serving. Serve with or without sugar according to taste.

Serves 8.

Ragi is locally made Indonesian yeast. One of my Australian friends has described the taste of this rice as similar to that of a light Old English Apple Cider. I included this recipe, having particularly in mind people going to Indonesia or Malaysia who are sure to be offered it sooner or later.

Rice Pancakes (Serabi)

250 g (2 cups) rice flour
½ teaspoon salt
1.5 litres lukewarm water
1 cup finely grated fresh coconut

2 candlenut kernels, ground
or
1 teaspoon ground almonds

Mix rice flour and salt in a basin. Make a well in the middle. Add water a little at a time and with back of a wooden spoon stir flour in gradually. Beat into a smooth batter. Add grated coconut and ground almonds to flour mixture and mix well. Allow to stand for an hour or so. Heat a small skillet, greased with a little oil. Pour ½ a ladle of mixture into skillet, cover and cook over a medium heat until the bottom is browned and small holes appear on top. The finished product is something like a crumpet in appearance. Repeat the process until the mixture is used up. Serve with the Coconut Milk Syrup, below.

Serves 8.

Coconut Milk Syrup

125 g (4 ounces) palm sugar,
   broken into very small pieces
4 cups coconut milk
1 piece cinnamon stick

1 7 cm (3-inch) piece of pandanus
   leaf (if available)
Pinch of salt

Place all ingredients in a saucepan and slowly bring to the boil, stirring all the time. Let simmer for 3 minutes. Strain through a piece of muslin into a bowl. Pour over individual helpings of Rice Pancakes while serving.

Steamed Coconut Custard (Serikaya)

1 cup water	6 eggs
125 g (4 ounces) Java brown sugar	Sugar
1 piece cinnamon stick	Pinch of salt
½ teaspoon aniseed	2 cups thick coconut milk
1 pandanus leaf (if available)	(type III)

Put water, Java sugar, cinnamon, aniseed and pandanus leaf in small saucepan over low heat until sugar dissolves. Put syrup through a piece of cheese-cloth. Cool slightly. Beat eggs and sugar until well blended in a large bowl, then add the coconut milk. Then pour in the cooled syrup gradually, stirring constantly. Pour custard mixture into 17.5 cm (7-inch) mould and steam until it sets right through. Or, place in a shallow pan of water. Bake in moderate oven 100°C (350°F) for about 45 minutes. The custard is set when a knife inserted near the centre comes out clean.

Serves 6.

Coconut Milk Layer Pudding (Kue lapis)

6 cups lukewarm thick coconut milk	1¼ cups sugar
1½ cups plain flour	2 teaspoons vanilla
2 rounded tablespoons	½ teaspoon salt
arrowroot flour	Few drops of cochineal

Mix coconut milk, the two sorts of flour, sugar, vanilla and salt thoroughly together. Divide into two equal parts. Leave one part white, to the other add a few drops of cochineal. Pour half the white mixture into a large rectangular or square dish or tin (say 23 cm [9 inches] by 23 cm [9 inches] by 5 cm [2 inches]) and steam until mixture is set. Then gently pour in half the pink mixture, taking care that it spreads evenly. Steam as above until firm. Then pour in the remaining white mixture and steam, and afterwards the remaining pink mixture and steam. You then have a four layer pudding. Cool to harden, before cutting into diamond or rectangular shapes with a thin sharp knife.

Serves 6.

Brown Sugar Layer Pudding (Kue talam)

FIRST MIXTURE

90 g (3 ounces) rice flour
185 g (6 ounces) cornflour
125 g (4 ounces) palm sugar
125 g (4 ounces) sugar

4 cups water
1 teaspoon aniseed
1 pandanus leaf (if available)
1 tablespoon margarine

SECOND MIXTURE

60 g (2 ounces) cornflour
60 g (2 ounces) rice flour

¼ teaspoon salt
2 cups coconut milk

I. Put rice and cornflour through a sieve into a large bowl. Dissolve brown sugar and sugar in water with aniseed and pandanus leaf added to it. Put syrup through a piece of muslin into a bowl. Then pour it slowly into the bowl with the flour in it. Mix to a smooth, fairly thin mixture. Stir in margarine, before pouring the mixture into a 30 cm (12-inch) steamer pan to be steamed. Stir the mixture while steaming until it thickens. As soon as it thickens, cover with greased paper and steam for another 10 minutes.

II. Sift cornflour and rice into a small bowl. Add salt. Pour coconut milk in the flour mixture in small quantity at a time, stirring well until mixture becomes smooth. Pour this mixture gently on top of first layer pudding which is still in the steamer. Cover and steam for about 15 minutes. Cool and cut into pie-shaped wedges. This pudding does not keep very long and if refrigerated becomes rubbery.

Yields 24 pieces.

Java Pudding (Puding Jawa)

250 g (8 ounces) brown sugar
1 cup water
3 eggs
250 g (8 ounces) flour
4 teaspoons instant coffee powder
½ teaspoon baking powder
185 g (6 ounces) butter
250 g (8 ounces) evaporated milk
  mixed with 2 cups water or
  fresh milk

½ teaspoon salt
2 teaspoons vanilla essence
60 g (2 ounces) raisins
60 g (2 ounces) sultanas
185 g (6 ounces) chopped nuts

Dissolve brown sugar in hot water. Strain if necessary and leave to cool. Beat eggs until fluffy. Sift flour, instant coffee powder and baking powder. Rub butter into flour mixture thoroughly. Then stir in milk, followed by brown sugar and beaten eggs. Mix well. Add salt and vanilla; then raisins, sultanas and chopped nuts into milk and flour mixture. Pour into a greased mould. Cover with greased paper and steam for 2½ hours.

Serves 8.

Agar-agar Coconut Pudding (Agar-agar serikaya)

8 g (¼ ounce) agar-agar or 2 cups soaked and drained agar-agar
5 cups water
1 cup brown sugar
1 teaspoon aniseed
1 small cinnamon stick

10 cm (4 inches) pandanas leaf (if available)
2 cups very thick coconut milk (type I)
¼ teaspoon salt
4 eggs, beaten

If using unsoaked agar-agar, soak it for an hour or longer. Boil soaked and drained agar-agar in water with sugar, aniseed, cinnamon stick and pandanus leaf till agar-agar dissolves, stirring occasionally. Add coconut milk and salt, bring again to boil. Stir continuously with down-up-over motion. Once mixture comes to boil, take it from the stove and pour through a piece of muslin into a bowl. Stir beaten eggs into agar-agar mixture and pour it into a 1 litre (2½-pint) mould. Let cool; then chill in the refrigerator. When the mixture sets, it forms two layers, a creamy upper layer on top and a plain lower one.

Serves 6.

Caramel Agar-agar (Agar-agar karamel)

½ cup water
1 cup sugar
8 g (¼ ounce) agar-agar or 2 cups soaked and drained agar-agar
5 cups water
½ cup sugar

2.5 cm (1-inch) piece vanilla pod
½ teaspoon salt
1 egg yolk
185 g (6 ounces) evaporated milk (1 small tin)
18 cm (7-inch) mould

If using unsoaked agar-agar, soak it an hour or longer. Cook water and sugar in small saucepan over low heat until sugar dissolves. Bring to boil and cook quickly until golden brown. Pour into 18 cm (7-inch) mould or 6 individual moulds. Hold with a cloth and quickly rotate mould till caramel coats side and base; if using individual moulds pour a little caramel into the base of each. Boil agar-agar in water with sugar and vanilla pod until agar-agar completely dissolves. Salt, and put through a piece of muslin. Mix egg yolk and milk in bowl. Stir the dissolved agar-agar into the milk and egg mixture and simmer for a few minutes, stirring all the time. Pour into prepared mould coated with caramel. Let cool, then chill in refrigerator for 2 hours or more before serving.

Serves 6.

Agar-agar Chocolate Pudding (Agar-agar coklat)

8 g ($\frac{1}{4}$ ounce) agar-agar
5 cups water
1 cup sugar
1 cup evaporated milk, undiluted
1 teaspoon vanilla

2 dessertspoons cocoa
$\frac{1}{2}$ cup hot water
$\frac{1}{4}$ teaspoon salt
4 eggs, separated

Boil soaked and drained agar-agar in water till it is all dissolved, stirring occasionally. Add sugar and when dissolved, add milk, stirring until it boils. Then add vanilla. Remove pan from cooker, strain through a piece of muslin into a bowl. Mix cocoa with hot water to make a smooth paste. Immediately add cocoa paste to the bowl and mix it in thoroughly. Finally fold in the 4 stiffly beaten egg whites and pour into mould. Let cool and chill in refrigerator. Serve with thin egg custard as sauce.

CUSTARD SAUCE

$\frac{1}{2}$ cup sugar
4 egg yolks
$\frac{1}{2}$ teaspoon cornflour

2 cups milk
$\frac{1}{2}$ teaspoon vanilla

Beat sugar and egg yolks until pale yellow. Beat in cornflour and gradually stir in milk. Pour mixture into top part of double saucepan over hot water and stir continuously until custard thickens. Remove from heat and keep on stirring for a minute to cool slightly. Pour into a jug.

Serves 6.

Pumpkin in Coconut Milk Syrup (Sanok)

750 g (1½ pounds) pumpkin
1½ cups water
¾ cup brown sugar
1 piece cinnamon stick
1 piece pandanus leaf, 10 cm
 (4-inches) long (if available)

¼ teaspoon salt
1 cup very thick coconut milk
 (type I)

Peel pumpkin and cut uniformly into 5 cm (2½-inch) chunks. Put aside. In a saucepan boil pumpkin in a mixture of water, brown sugar, flavoured with cinnamon and pandanus leaf and salt until tender. Check by piercing with a skewer. Add coconut milk and bring back to boil, stirring constantly to prevent coconut milk from curdling. Serve hot or at room temperature, by itself or with Boiled Glutinous Rice (*Ketan*, p. 24).

Serves 5.

Instead of adding coconut milk, the pumpkin can simply be served with beaten fresh cream. Sweet potatoes and bananas may be also cooked this way.

Avocadoes

Is the avocado pear fruit or vegetable? Of course, it is fruit, but it can play the role of either. In this country it is often seasoned or teamed up elegantly with a shell-fish salad and served as a first course. In Indonesia, on the other hand, it is treated solely as a fruit and is served after the meal.

Cut avocado into two halves. Remove stone; scoop out the avocado flesh with melon-ball cutter. Sprinkle with lemon juice and brown sugar. Serve in individual serving bowls as a dessert.

Avocado Whip (Eskrim pokat)

1 avocado
Juice of 1 lemon
2 tablespoons sugar

1 cup (8 ounces) vanilla
 ice cream

Cut fruit in half lengthwise, and gently prize out stone. Peel and mash flesh, and put through a sieve. Add lemon juice and sugar. Combine avocado mixture and ice cream and whip with rotary beater until smooth. Place in freezer to chill, but do not freeze.

Serves 4.

13 Cakes and Biscuits

THE MONTH of Ramadhan is one of rigorous penitence, when quarrels are made up, grudges are forgotten, and everyone resolves to make a fresh start. The festival celebrating the end of the fasting month is one of great happiness and excitement. The day is greeted by a vigorous beating on the mosque drum, and everyone is astir early to have everything ready to celebrate the great festival of *Id al-Fitr,* the ending of the fast, one of the greatest days in the year for Muslims throughout the world.

In fact, preparations have been going on for the previous fortnight. The womenfolk have been cooking biscuits of as many as twenty different kinds or more, and storing them decoratively in attractive, tightly-closed glass jars; plus of course a few cakes and one elaborately decorated as an accent to be placed on the table as the centrepiece.

As the day draws closer, they prepare the principal meat dishes. In the evenings they are busy sewing, for everyone must have new clothes. By the time the mosque drum signals the great day, peoples' homes are all bulging with food and the biscuits and cakes which have been hidden away in every conceivable place in cupboards, on shelves, even up in the rafters, are all brought down and displayed on a special table. The display is meant to be attractive to look at, with the biscuit jars arranged symmetrically according to size, but it is also a labour saving device. For when, after the outdoor congregational prayer, everyone holds open house and visitors stream in, only tea, coffee or soft drinks need to be served and guests can make their own choice from the variety of confections before them.

I have taken this season of the year as a lead into the section on biscuits and cakes because it is the time when people really go to town preparing them, whether they are of local style, Dutch style, or a blend of the two. Neither my grandmother nor my mother had any cookery books to which they could refer. The only measures they had were teacups, glasses and spoons; for the rest, they went by smell, taste and some kind of sixth sense. As far as I know, they had no failures. They could only have learnt their skills by hard work and patience, yet this cooking was something they enjoyed, for they were doing it for loved ones and friends, some of whom they may not have seen for many months, if not years. This is because everyone who possibly can returns to his family home for this festival to meet kinsfolk and old friends again. In fact, people return literally in their thousands, and some villages which, for the rest of the year are half-deserted and inhabited only by the old folk, return to life and bustle with activity.

Like Christmas, it is particularly a time for children. On the village green there is often a fair and the night is noisy and lit up with fire-works. In some areas it is traditional for children to be rewarded with a few cents for every male relative and acquaintance whose hand they take in greeting saying, 'Selamat Hari Raya, ma'af lahir batin', (a happy feast to you; please pardon all my faults).

Of course, biscuits and cakes are served with tea to afternoon visitors all through the year, but not on the same scale and they usually come from the bakers. The following recipes are a selection from those which are popular throughout Indonesia, some of them local and traditional, others Dutch in origin.

Spiced Rich Layer Cake (Spekkoek)

It is not possible to cook this cake successfully unless the oven has two elements, a bottom element and a grill element at the top.

500 g (1 pound) butter
350 g (11¼ ounces) castor sugar
18 egg yolks
6 egg whites
350 g (11¼ ounces) plain flour,
  sieved
1½ teaspoons ground nutmeg

1½ teaspoons ground mace
½ teaspoon ground cloves
2 teaspoons ground cinnamon
1½ teaspoons ground cardamon
2 teaspoons vanilla

Line the bottom of a 23 cm (9 inch) tin with greaseproof paper. Grease with melted butter and dust lightly with flour. Set the oven temperature at moderate: 180°C (350°F). Cream butter with one-third of the sugar until light and creamy. Beat egg yolks with one-third of the sugar until creamy. Put egg whites in a bowl and beat well; add the balance of the sugar and continue beating until stiff. Add beaten egg yolks to the butter mixture, fold in flour, the spices (sieved) and vanilla, then fold in egg whites and mix thoroughly. Spoon 4 tablespoons of mixture into the tin, spread it evenly and bake for 15 minutes or until it is cooked. Brush the baked layer with butter and press lightly all over with the flat bottom of a glass. If any bubble appears prick it with a toothprick. For the second layer, scoop 3 tablespoons of mixture on to the first layer, spread it evenly and place the cake tin the middle rack and bake the cake for about 3 minutes under the top element set on low. Add and bake the following layers in the same way until the mixture is finished, using the heat from the top element in the oven. Be sure to brush with butter and press lightly with the flat bottom of the glass after each layer is baked before adding new mixture. This mixture should produce about 11 layers. Let cool on wire rack. Since the cake is very rich, serve in thin square slices.

How to slice the spiced layer cake: You need a sharp knife with a thin blade. First cut a circle about 5 cm (2 inches) from the edge of the cake using a saucer to guide the knife. When serving, first cut the outer circle into 1 cm (½-inch) slices. This produces small, convenient-sized pieces, 40 to 50 slices, and also shows off the visual effect of the layers in the inner circle and the ends of the outer circle. This cake will keep up to two weeks if placed in a tin.

Marble Cake (Tar marmer)

250 g (½ pound) butter
2 cups castor sugar
6 eggs, separated
3 cups self-raising flour
Pinch of salt
1 teaspoon mixed spice

1 cup milk
1 teaspoon vanilla
2 tablespoons cocoa dissolved in
    4 tablespoons boiling water

Brush a deep 23 cm (9-inch) cake tin with melted butter and then with flour. Shake off any surplus of flour. Cream butter with two-thirds of the sugar until light and creamy. Add egg yolks one at a time and beat well. Beat egg whites until stiff, add the remaining one-third of sugar. Continue beating until sugar is dissolved. Fold in whites, then sifted flour, salt, vanilla and mixed spice into creamed mixture alternately with milk. Divide mixture into two equal parts, white and chocolate, by adding dissolved cocoa. Pour alternate layers of white and chocolate mixture into prepared tin. Run a spoon through cake using a circular movement to blend the colours slightly, producing a marble-like effect. Bake in a preheated oven at 180°C (350°F) for about 50-60 minutes. Turn cake out; when cool, decorate as desired.

Banana Cake (Cake pisang)

½ cup milk
2 tablespoons lemon juice
250 g (8 ounces) butter
1 cup castor sugar
2 eggs

3 large bananas, mashed
2 cups flour
1 teaspoon baking powder
1 teaspoon bicarbonate of soda
½ teaspoon salt

Brush a deep 20 cm (8-inch) cake tin with melted butter. Set oven temperature at a moderate 180°C (350°F). Mix the milk and lemon juice, put aside. Cream butter and sugar until light and creamy. Add the eggs, one at a time, to creamed mixture and beat well. To this add the milk and lemon mixture and the mashed banana. Blend well. Sift flour, baking powder, bicarbonate of soda and salt and fold into the mixture. Pour mixture into prepared tin and bake in moderate oven for 50-60 minutes. Cool on a wire rack.

Banana Orange Cake (Cake pisang pakai air jeruk)

250 g (8 ounces) butter
1 cup castor sugar
4 eggs, separated
3 bananas, mashed

2 cups self-raising flour
½ teaspoon bicarbonate of soda
¼ teaspoon salt
Juice of 1 orange, strained

Brush a 20 cm (8-inch) fluted ring tin with melted butter and dust lightly with flour. Set oven temperature at a moderate 180°C (350°F). Cream butter and sugar until light and creamy. Add egg yolks, one at a time and beat well, and to this add mashed banana. Blend well. Sift flour, bicarbonate of soda and salt, and fold into creamed mixture alternately with orange juice. Lastly fold in the stiffly beaten egg whites and pour mixture immediately into prepared tin; bake in moderate oven for 40-45 minutes. Cool on a wire rack.

Cinnamon Stick Biscuits (Kue batang cengkeh)

2½ cups plain flour
½ cup cornflour
250 g (8 ounces) butter
1 cup castor sugar

2 egg yolks
1 teaspoon ground cinnamon
60 g (2 ounces) sugar
60 g (2 ounces) ground almonds

Sift plain flour and cornflour into a bowl. Rub in butter until mixture resembles breadcrumbs. Stir in sugar, then work into a dough with beaten egg yolks and ground cinnamon, adding a little water if necessary. Chill. Meanwhile mix sugar and ground almonds well. Take small pieces of dough and mould into sticks about 5 cm (2 inches) long and 4 mm ($\frac{1}{4}$ inch) thick. Dip in ground almond mixture. Place on buttered baking tray and bake in a moderate oven at 180°C (350°F) for 15-20 minutes.

Cats Tongue Biscuits (Kue lidah kucing)

$1\frac{1}{2}$ cups arrowroot flour
$1\frac{1}{2}$ cups self-raising flour
6 egg whites

250 g ($\frac{1}{2}$ pound) icing sugar
250 g ($\frac{1}{2}$ pound) butter
$\frac{1}{2}$ teaspoon vanilla essence

Some recipes require only egg yolks. These biscuits are an ideal, simple way of using up leftover whites.
Sift arrowroot and self-raising flour together. Beat egg whites until stiff. Sprinkle half the sugar on top and beat until sugar is dissolved. Cream butter with balance of sugar and vanilla. When creamy and smooth, fold in beaten egg whites and then the flour mixture. Using biscuit press, make oblong shapes of the mixture and place on a greased baking tray leaving spaces between each. Bake in a moderate preheated oven at 180°C (350°F) until light golden (about 15 minutes).

Coconut Biscuits (Kue kelapa)

125 g (4 ounces) butter
$\frac{1}{2}$ cup sugar
2 eggs

1 cup self-raising flour
125 g ($\frac{1}{4}$ pound) desiccated coconut
1 teaspoon vanilla essence

Cream butter and sugar. Add eggs one at a time and beat until light. Then fold in flour. Add desiccated coconut and vanilla and stir well. Drop small teaspoonfuls on to a greased baking tray, allowing room to spread, and bake in moderate oven at 180°C (350°F) for 20-30 minutes.

Index